THE ROYAL AUSTRALIAN NAVY
IN WORLD WAR II

THE ROYAL AUSTRALIAN NAVY IN WORLD WAR II

Edited by David Stevens

ALLEN & UNWIN

This book is dedicated to the memory of all those who became casualties while serving in the RAN or WRANS during the period of hostilities (3 September 1939 to 15 August 1945).

First published in 1996
Allen & Unwin Pty Ltd
9 Atchison St, St Leonards, NSW 2065 Australia

Phone: (61 2) 9901 4088
Fax: (61 2) 9906 2218
E-mail: 100252.103@compuserve.com

National Library of Australia
Cataloguing-in-Publication entry:

The Royal Australian Navy in World War II:
essays on the Australian experience in naval war.

Includes index.
ISBN 1 86448 035 1.

1. Australia. Royal Australian Navy—History—World
War, 1939–1945. 2. World War, 1939–1945—Naval
operations, Australian. I. Stevens, David, 1958– .

940.545994

Set in 10/12 pt Times by DOCUPRO, Sydney
Printed by Ligare Pty Ltd, Sydney

10 9 8 7 6 5 4 3 2 1

Foreword

Australia is, and always has been, a maritime nation. From the earliest days of European settlement, the people of Australia have looked to the sea for their security. Protection was first provided under the umbrella of Imperial Defence and the Royal Navy. Later, as our nation matured, the need was identified to establish an Australian Navy, manned and commanded by Australians. Formed ten years after Federation, the proud fighting traditions of the Royal Australian Navy owe much to the courage and sacrifice displayed by earlier generations. The RAN, its officers and sailors, both permanent and reserves, have often been at the forefront of encounters with an enemy.

World War II embraced history's greatest naval conflict and Allied victory was ultimately due to the skilful exercise of maritime power. Although not among the largest of the participants, our Navy was fully involved throughout the six years of war, serving around the globe and in an enormous variety of tasks. From escorting convoys in the Atlantic to minesweeping in Bass Strait, from single-ship actions in the Red Sea to the great sea battle of Leyte Gulf, Australian ships and personnel were at work.

The Navy does not exist in a vacuum but functions as part of a wider defence organisation maintaining the security of our country. The scale and associated risk of maritime operations vary widely between times of peace and war. The Australian Navy at the beginning of World War II provides a prime example. In September 1939, the RAN had some 5500 men and 15 ships, with another three under construction. Significantly, on the day following the declaration of war, the Australian Squadron was already at sea, patrolling off the New South Wales coast, while other ships were on station in the Indian and Atlantic Oceans. Mobilisation began immediately. By June 1945, at the RAN's peak strength there were 337 ships and 39 650 serving men and women—80 per cent of them reservists.

Though Australians have a tendency to think more of the casualties incurred during land campaigns, the RAN's losses at sea have at times also been tragically high. Between 1939 and 1945, more than 2000 naval men and women gave their lives in the service of their country; a higher percentage death rate than that suffered by either of the other two services. In November 1941, Australia's single biggest civil or military disaster occurred when the cruiser HMAS *Sydney* was lost with all hands. This tragic event took place just 100 miles off the Australian coast and in 1994 became the first national commemorative event on the Federal Government's 'Australia Remembers 1945–95' Program.

This book highlights the work of the Navy as part of Australia's wider achievements as an independent nation. It reflects a welcome trend in the study of our naval history, to cover a wider and more varied area of the rich historical fabric of the RAN. This is a timely opportunity to tell all Australians something of our naval heritage and, in so doing, to increase community awareness of the contribution the Navy has made to our national development in the past, and the potential it has to do so in the future.

Importantly, this volume also goes some way towards commemorating all those naval men and women, who served both at sea and on the home front, during World War II. It is in part an acknowledgment of the debt we owe them for their unselfish actions in a time of severe adversity. I commend this story to all Australians.

Vice Admiral R.G. Taylor AO RAN
Chief of Naval Staff

Contents

Illustrations

Maps

Tables and figures

Tables

Figures

Abbreviations

AA	Anti-aircraft
ABDA	Australian–British–Dutch–American
ACNB	Australian Commonwealth Naval Board
ACNS	Assistant Chief of the Naval Staff
ADFA	Australian Defence Force Academy
ADM	Admiralty
AMS	Australian Minesweeper
ANMM	Australian National Maritime Museum
AOC	Air Officer Commanding
A/S	Anti-Submarine
ASIS	Australian Secret Intelligence Service
ASW	Anti-Submarine Warfare
AWAS	Australian Women's Army Service
AWM	Australian War Memorial
BPF	British Pacific Fleet
CinC	Commander-in-Chief
CINCPAC	CinC Pacific
CANFSWPA	Commander Allied Naval Forces South-West Pacific Area
CAPT	Captain
CCAS	Commodore Commanding the Australian Squadron
CCS	Combined Chiefs of Staff
CID	Committee for Imperial Defence
CMDR	Commander
CNO	Chief of Naval Operations
CNS	Chief of the Naval Staff
CO	Commanding Officer
COIC	Combined Operational Intelligence Centre
COMINCH	Commander-in-Chief

CSS	Commonwealth Security Service
CTF	Commander Task Force
CTG	Commander Task Group
CTU	Commander Task Unit
D/F	Direction finding
DNI	Director of Naval Intelligence
DSC	Distinguished Service Cross
DSM	Distinguished Service Medal
FELO	Far Eastern Liaison Office
GC	George Cross
GHQ	General Headquarters
GM	George Medal
GOC	General Officer Commanding
HDML	Harbour Defence Motor Launch
HMAS	His Majesty's Australian Ship
HMS	His Majesty's Ship
IJN	Imperial Japanese Navy
JCS	Joint Chiefs of Staff
IWM	Imperial War Museum
LCDR	Lieutenant-Commander
LEUT	Lieutenant
NID	Naval Intelligence Division
MID	Mentioned in Dispatches
NA	National Archives
NOIC	Naval Officer-in-Charge
OBE	Order of the British Empire
PLENAPS	Plans for the Employment of Naval and Air Forces of the Associated Powers in the Eastern Theatre
PNF	Permanent Naval Forces
PRO	Public Records Office
RAAF	Royal Australian Air Force
RACAS	Rear-Admiral Commanding the Australian Squadron
RADM	Rear-Admiral
RAN	Royal Australian Navy
RANC	Royal Australian Naval College
RANR	Royal Australian Navy Reserve
RANVR	Royal Australian Navy Volunteer Reserve
RCN	Royal Canadian Navy
RN	Royal Navy
RNR	Royal Navy Reserve
RNVR	Royal Navy Volunteer Reserve
RNZN	Royal New Zealand Navy
ROP	Reports of Proceedings

Abbreviations

SAG	Surface Action Group
SBLT	Sub-Lieutenant
SMB	Survey Motor Boat
SNOWA	Senior Naval Officer Western Australia
SWPA	South-West Pacific Area
SWPSF	South-West Pacific Sea Frontiers
TF	Task Force
TG	Task Group
TU	Task Unit
USFIA	United States Forces in Australia
USN	United States Navy
USNI	United States Naval Institute
USS	United States Ship
VADM	Vice-Admiral
VC	Victoria Cross
VNESAD	Voluntary National Emergency Service Ambulance Drivers
WAAAF	Women's Auxiliary Australian Air Force
WESC	Women's Emergency Signal Corps
WNS	Women's Naval Service
WRANS	Women's Royal Australian Naval Service
WRENS	Women's Reserve Emergency Naval Service
WRNS	Women's Royal Naval Service

Notes on contributors

J.G. Betty

On completion of his civil engineering degree John Betty enlisted as a SBLT in the RANVR in December 1943. During 1944–45 he saw service in New Guinea, in the Philippines and in northern Australian waters in HMA Ships *Moresby* and *Warrego*. When hostilities ceased, *Warrego* engaged in reoccupation of the former Dutch East Indies followed by a survey in Yampi Sound. Early in 1946, John Betty was appointed in command of HMAS *Jabiru*. Following demobilisation in March 1947, he resumed his civil engineering career. He maintained his association with the sea through his interest in coastal engineering and marine structures and was a foundation member of the national Committee on Coastal Engineering from 1973 until his retirement. His manual, *Engineering Contracts*, was published in 1993 by McGraw-Hill.

Associate Professor F. Broeze

Frank Broeze immigrated from the Netherlands in 1970. He is president of the International Commission of Maritime History and deputy chair, Board of the Western Australian Maritime Museum. He has taught, researched and written extensively on many aspects of maritime history, including imperial history, naval strategy and maritime ideology. His particular interests include geopolitics, social history and biography. He is committed to integrate maritime and naval history into general Australian history and to place Australian history in its regional and international context. At present he is working on a book, *Maritime Australia: A History of Australians and the Sea*.

J.D. Brown

David Brown was born in England in 1938. After serving as an observer in the RN from 1957–69 he joined the Ministry of Defence's Naval Historical Branch. He became its head in 1977 and was later dual-hatted as assistant director (data and doctrine) in the Naval Staff Duties Division of the Naval Staff. He is the author of many books and monographs, particularly on naval aviation. Co-author of the *Guinness Book of Air Warfare*, one of his major works is *The Royal Navy and the Falklands War*. He was recently elected a Fellow of the Royal Historical Society.

Lieutenant A. Cooper, RAN

Alastair Cooper joined the RAN in 1988. He graduated from the Australian Defence Force Academy (ADFA) with a BA(Hons) in 1991 and qualified as a seaman officer in 1994. He has served in patrol boats and frigates and is currently posted to HMAS *Canberra* as an officer of the watch. His research interests include Australian military and economic history and the development of naval warfare.

Dr C. Coulthard-Clark

Chris Coulthard-Clark is a professional historian and is currently engaged as a consultant to write a history of Australian Defence Industries Ltd. Several of his numerous books have had Australian naval themes, including *Action Stations Coral Sea* and *The Shame of Savo* (with Bruce Loxton), as well as several papers published in Australia and the United States. His volume of the official war history series, dealing with RAAF involvement in Vietnam, was published in 1995.

Dr I. Cowman

Ian Cowman was educated at the University of Queensland and King's College London. He is a historian and naval and military specialist, and is the author of the forthcoming, *Dominion or Decline: Anglo–American naval relations in the Pacific 1937–41*. He has also published several articles on British and American naval policy both before and during World War II. At the moment he is writing a monograph on the early history of the RAN entitled *'A Vision Splendid': Australia, Naval Strategy and Empire 1900–23*, and is researching a sequel on Anglo–American naval relations 1941–45.

Commander J.V.P. Goldrick, RAN

James Goldrick joined the RANC in 1974. He holds BA and M.Litt. degrees and is an anti-submarine warfare specialist who has seen sea service with the RAN and on exchange with the RN. He has served as aide-de-camp to the Governor-General and as research officer to CNS. Command of HMAS *Cessnock* was followed by a year as an international research fellow at the US Naval War College at Newport. Prior to taking up his current appointment as executive officer HMAS *Perth,* Commander Goldrick was in charge of the RAN's Principle Warfare Officer Training and Tactical Development Unit at the RAN Surface Warfare School, HMAS *Watson*. Publications include *The King's Ships Were at Sea*, and a variety of edited books, as well as many articles on contemporary and historical naval subjects.

Commander A.W. Grazebrook, RANR

Tony Grazebrook will shortly complete 43 years service as a naval reservist. In civilian life he is a defence journalist and farmer. He has written for defence magazines since 1974. Currently, he is editor of *Australian–Pacific Defence Reporter* and Australian correspondent for the British naval newsletter *NAVINT*. He writes regularly on contemporary defence, defence industry and naval affairs. Naval history has been a lifelong interest and previous works include papers on 'Rear Admiral H.B. Farncombe', 'Fleet Admiral King and other Pacific Admirals', 'The Young Turks', 'The Ottoman Navy', and 'The First Admiral: A Biography of Admiral Sir Francis Hyde'.

E.J. Grove

Eric Grove joined the History Department at Britannia RNC, Dartmouth, as a civilian lecturer in 1971. In 1980–81 he was exchange professor at the US Naval Academy, Annapolis. Leaving Dartmouth as Deputy Head of Strategic Studies in 1984, he worked for a year with the Council of Arms Control and then became a freelance defence analyst and naval historian. He has taught at the RNC Greenwich and Cambridge University, was a research fellow at the University of Southampton and was consultant for the National Maritime Museum's new Sea Power gallery. He also helped set up the Foundation for International Security and, under its auspices, initiated the Adderbury Talks, annual discussions between the RN, USN and Russian Navy. His many books and articles include, *Vanguard to Trident: British Naval Policy since World War II*, *The Future of Sea Power* and *Fleet to Fleet Encounters*. Since October 1993 he has been Lecturer in International Politics at the University of Hull, where he is also Deputy Director of the Centre for Security Studies.

M.C. Hordern

Marsden Hordern joined the RAN in 1942. Service from 1942–45 included convoy duties and time in Fairmiles. After two years at sea as a junior officer he was appointed to command HDML *1347*. He commissioned and fitted her out in Sydney, took her to the north of Dutch New Guinea, and after the war brought her back to Australia and paid her off in Brisbane in 1946. From 1947–70 he was a member of the RANR and RNR. His first book, *Mariners are Warned*, the story of HMS *Beagle*'s survey of Australian waters 1837–43, was published in 1989. The book won the *Age* 'Book of the Year Award', the Victorian Government's 'Literary Prize' and the inaugural prize awarded by the ANMM for Australian Maritime History. He is now writing a companion book on the discoveries and hydrographic work of Phillip Parker King, 1817–22.

Commodore B. Loxton, RAN (Rtd)

Bruce Loxton joined the RANC in 1938. As a midshipman he was seriously wounded on the bridge of HMAS *Canberra* when the cruiser was disabled during the opening stages of the battle of Savo Island. Before retiring from the RAN in 1978 he had commanded three ships and served, among other positions, as

Director of Naval Intelligence and Australian Naval Attache, Washington. He is a graduate of the RAN Staff College, the US Naval War College and the Royal College of Defence Studies. His first book, *The Shame of Savo* (with Chris Coulthard-Clark) was published in 1994.

Lieutenant J.S. Sears, RAN

Jason Sears entered the RAN as part of the first intake into ADFA in 1985 and graduated with a first class honours degree in history in 1989. Since that time he has served as deputy supply officer in HMA Ships *Torrens* and *Adelaide,* and research officer to CNS. He is currently undertaking PhD studies in history at ADFA. His thesis topic is 'A Social History of the Officers of the Royal Australian Navy, 1911–50'.

K. Spurling

Kathryn Spurling joined the WRANS in 1966 and left the service at the end of 1968. In 1988 she graduated from UNSW with a masters degree in history (hons) with a thesis titled 'The Women's Royal Australian Naval Service: A study in discrimination 1939–60'. She has subsequently published several articles relating to the utilisation of servicewomen throughout the world. In 1989 she was a member of an ADFA research team engaged to produce a background paper for the RAN Officer Career Study. Since 1989 she has been research assistant to Professor David Day on the history of the Australian Customs Department. The first volume of this work, *Smugglers and Sailors*, was published in 1992 and the second volume will be published shortly.

D.M. Stevens

David Stevens is the Director of Naval Historical Studies within the RAN's Maritime Studies Program. He joined the RANC in 1974 as a junior entry cadet midshipman. In 1984 he undertook warfare training in the UK and later served as the anti-submarine warfare officer in HMA Ships *Yarra* and *Hobart* and on exchange in HMS *Hermione*. In 1990–91 he served on the staff of the Australian Task Group Commander during Operation DAMASK and the 1991 Gulf War. His last naval posting was with the ANZAC Ship Project. He graduated from the ANU in 1992 with a MA (Strategic Studies). He has written articles of naval historical interest for a number of newspapers and professional journals.

J. H. Straczek

Joe Straczek joined the RAN as a junior recruit in 1971. He was appointed a midshipman in the Supply Branch in 1977. On completion of his specialist training he undertook a number of Supply-related postings. He completed the RAN Staff Course in 1988. After 20 years' service, Lieutenant Commander Straczek resigned his commission to take up the position of Senior Naval Historical and Archives officer within the Department of Defence (Navy). He has contributed articles on Australian naval history to a number of journals.

B. Winter

Barbara Winter is an author writing on naval and military historical themes and specialising in Intelligence aspects, including cryptanalysis. As a linguist and former teacher of languages, she is able to access foreign language material that has not been translated into English, or has been translated badly. Two of her previous books dealt with the sinking of HMAS *Sydney* and German prisoners of war in Australia. Her book on naval intelligence in Australia, and the role played by the Director of Naval Intelligence, Commander Rupert Long, was published by Boolarong in 1995.

Conversion table

1 inch	=	25.4 millimetres
1 yard	=	0.9144 metre
1 (statute) mile	=	1.609 kilometres
1 (nautical) mile	=	1.852 kilometres
1 acre	=	0.405 hectare
1 pound (weight)	=	0.4536 kilogram
1 gallon	=	4.546 litres
1 shilling	=	10 cents
1 pound (currency)	=	2 dollars

Introduction

David Stevens

The year 1995 marked the fiftieth anniversary of the end of World War II and today's Australians were encouraged to take part in a series of events under the auspices of the Federal Government's 'Australia Remembers 1945–95' Program. For many young Australians, understanding of war centres on the experience of Gallipoli in 1915 and the start of the ANZAC legend. Yet it was during World War II that Australia first truly came under direct enemy threat, and many more Australians gained first-hand knowledge of conflict between 1939 and 1945 than in 1914–18. The Australia Remembers Program aimed to give every Australian the opportunity to remember those who served in the armed services or on the home front during the war, commemorate those who lost their lives, think of those who lost loved ones and celebrate fifty years of peace. As a major element of its contribution to events the Royal Australian Navy held a conference, 'The RAN in World War II'. The conference aimed to take a fresh and critical look at the part the service played during the war. This book originated at that conference and is now presented to a wider audience.

Many books have been published on the exploits of individual Australian ships during World War II and on specific battles. But the story of the Navy at war involves much more than narratives of brief but fierce engagements. It must also include the broad issues of strategy and naval policy, the vital but often monotonous duties of escort and patrol, and the involvement of the wider Australian community, including industry. A navy is also 'a living thing' comprised not only of equipment but people. The very real fears and triumphs of ordinary young men and women must be considered. The contributions that follow were selected because they bring a new perspective to accounts of the RAN at war. It is not necessarily a matter of 'rewriting' history, though some past errors are corrected, but often a matter of gaining recognition for areas long neglected. Moreover, the authors have dealt with analysis as well as description and therefore the book serves to deepen the understanding of our naval history, in addition to improving the existing coverage.

A book such as this cannot hope to cover all aspects of the RAN's experience during the war. Many courageous and significant exploits by individuals and groups have by necessity been left out. Their exclusion does not mean these incidents were in any way less worthy of recognition, but simply that the RAN's contribution to the war effort encompassed such a vast array of important areas. It is not commonly realised, for example, that some 20 per cent of those anti-submarine personnel who served during the critical Battle of the Atlantic were trained in Australia. One particular Australian, Stan Darling, an RANVR officer serving with the RN, as commanding officer of HMS *Loch Killen*, was responsible for the destruction of three U-boats. On the other side of the world it was the Australian warship HMAS *Diamantina* that accepted the surrender of the central Pacific island of Ocean, the last British Empire outpost in Japanese hands, on 1 October 1945. This final ceremony came almost a month after the official Japanese surrender in Tokyo Bay.

This book can only offer a few brief scenes from a substantially greater canvas. Much more remains to be said and many other stories still remain untold. Readers who wish to find out more are directed in the first instance to the two-volume *Royal Australian Navy 1939–45*, by George Hermon Gill. Often regarded as the best of the official history series, nothing rivals Gill's sweeping account of what each Australian warship did in the war—where they steamed and fought, and with what result. More detailed sources can be found in the notes at the end of this book.

Acknowledgments

This book is the result of a joint effort, support and practical assistance being willingly given by a wide variety of people and organisations. Recognition must first go to the contributors, who worked hard to provide many new and revealing insights into the RAN at war.

The 1995 Naval History Conference was co-hosted by the RAN's Maritime Studies Program, the Australian Naval Institute and the Australian National Maritime Museum. The Naval Historical Society of Australia and the Department of Veterans' Affairs, 'Australia Remembers 1945–95 Task Force', also provided assistance, while the Minister for Veterans' Affairs, the Honourable Con Sciacca, kindly agreed to open the event. Acknowledgment must also include the conference sponsors LOPAC Pty Ltd, Australian Defence Industries Pty Ltd and Graeme Dunk Consulting.

All those who participated at the conference receive my sincere thanks. The presence of a large number of World War II veterans allowed personal experiences to enliven and improve the quality of proceedings. Appreciation is likewise due to Rear-Admiral David Campbell, Rear-Admiral Chris Oxenbould, Commodore

Naval Staff (CNS) in particular, who were also forced to spend much time in transit between Canberra and Melbourne. Furthermore, coordination with the seagoing forces suffered from the fact that the Australian Squadron's principal operational base was Sydney.

Even the reorganisation of the Defence Department in November 1939 proved a mixed blessing. The three services and supply were moved into new, individual departments under a new Department of Defence Coordination.[2] The benefit was that this gave the Navy its own Minister once more. The key weakness was that it made even more tenuous the RAN's influence on the highest levels of policy by removing one of the direct links with the Minister of Defence, who was no longer ex-officio president of the ACNB.

There were other factors. Between 1937 and 1948, the First Naval Member and CNS was a senior officer on loan from the RN. The same applied to the Second Naval Member/Chief of Naval Personnel until 1942 and the Flag Officer Commanding the Australian Squadron until 1944. These officers required time to adapt themselves to local conditions and achieve the confidence of the government.[3]

The final constraint related to force structure. Although the Navy had consistently received the lion's share of the limited defence vote between the wars, this was never sufficient to support a capital ship after the disposal of the battle cruiser HMAS *Australia* in 1924. Consequently, Australia's naval forces were configured to conduct trade protection and local defence, and to provide reinforcements for the British fleet when it arrived in Singapore. While the emphasis placed on these roles had varied over the years, proposals for a capital ship[4] had been overtaken by events and the mixed force of cruisers and destroyers that entered the war was incapable of independent operations against any large-scale threat. This put the RAN at the margins of strategic decision-making within the government.

The results of these constraints were that the strategy under which the RAN operated was always received by or imposed upon it, and that long-term policy development was essentially personal. The senior advisers available to the CNS were few in number and limited in experience.[5] Without the creative energies of an active CNS, little forward planning for the Navy as a military force could be conducted, however efficient the logistic and administrative arrangements.

Phase 1: Containing Germany

The ACNB monitored events in 1939 with increasing anxiety, taking cues directly from the Admiralty to advance preparations for war. Britain and France appeared capable of matching Germany and the greatest threat to Australia was likely to be surface commerce raiders. On the other hand, either Italy or Japan might take advantage of the situation. The Naval Board had thus to balance commitment to

Members of the Australian Commonwealth Naval Board in 1941. From left to right: R. Anthony, Finance Member; Engineer Rear-Admiral P.E. McNeil, Third Naval Member; Admiral Sir Ragnar Colvin, retiring First Naval Member; G.L. Macandie, Secretary Naval Board; Vice-Admiral Sir Guy Royle, First Naval Member; A.R. Nankervis, Secretary, Department of Navy Member; Commodore J.W. Durnford, Second Naval Member; H.G. Brain, Business Member. (AWM 128093)

the Imperial effort with provision for regional defence in the event of Japan's entering the war.

The principal question was not whether RAN ships would comply with the British War Telegram when the latter was issued, but what Australian forces could be spared, Cabinet taking a much harder line than the ACNB.[6] On 30 August, all RAN units were transferred to Admiralty control, but with the stipulation that 'no ships (other than the newly commissioned cruiser HMAS *Perth*, lent to the British in the West Indies) should be taken from Australian waters without prior concurrence of the Australian Government'.[7] The Admiralty immediately raised the ante with a sudden request for destroyers. Annoyed at the use of naval channels for what should have been an inter-government matter[8], Cabinet required some persuasion before the ships were sent. The remaining major units of the Australian Squadron were employed on focal area operations, while newly commissioned ships worked up.

The activities of German raiders in the Indian Ocean and South Atlantic remained a threat, particularly as individual RAN cruisers were no match for pocket battleships, and concern mounted with the prospect of the passage of the first troop convoy to the Middle East. The Admiralty met this by attaching a battleship to the escort force and providing reliefs for the Australian cruisers before they strayed too far from local waters.

These first months of the war were otherwise relatively quiet in Australian waters. While port defences were progressively developed, with particular attention to Sydney, Fremantle and Darwin, local requisitioned patrol and minesweeping craft were worked up to a reasonable degree of efficiency. Despite initial concerns over the possibility of submarine attack, it soon became evident that the relatively small U-boat force was confining its activities to northern Europe and the focus for local defence therefore remained on surface raiders.

The war curtailed rather than expanded the RAN's plans for force development. Construction of major warships in Australia would draw too heavily on the limited finance and available local industrial capacity when the Army and the Air Force had more pressing claims. The RAN now had to wait its turn, a situation recognised as early as 1938.[9] With six cruisers available, five of which were relatively modern, there was no immediate argument for expansion at this level, and naval priorities turned to escort and minesweeping forces.

The key element was the *Bathurst* class Australian minesweeper (AMS) designed to provide a ship capable of both minesweeping and long-range escort.[10] The essentially uncomplicated design of the *Bathursts* allowed production without delays from equipment lost on passage from the United Kingdom, unlike the destroyers already building.[11] Moderation was the right approach. Progress in defence industry was to prove erratic and slow, retarded not only by the restrictions in available funding but by the technological demands of weapons production. For the Navy the problem was exacerbated by the relative complexity of its equipment and its inevitable surrender of priority to the other services.

Personnel expansion was managed through the mechanism of the Volunteer Reserve. 'Hostilities Only' officers and ratings were employed, additional to the permanent establishment. This was intended to avoid repetition of the massive retrenchment of 1919–23 by constraining increases in career personnel to peacetime requirements. It had the merit of simplicity, but laid up a store of problems for the end of the war, when the attempt would be made to organise the RAN on an expanded basis and with more sophisticated and manpower-intensive ships.

Phase 2: A situation out of control

The fall of France and Italy's entry to the war destroyed the last hopes of sustaining the defence strategy of the previous twenty years. Significantly, the British decision to remain in the Mediterranean came as a surprise to the Australian naval staff, which had applied the arithmetic of the limited force levels to include the Far East but not the Middle Sea.[12] The dangerous implications of this step were made clear in June when the British finally admitted that it was

Figure 1.1: Australian Commonwealth Naval Board, November 1939

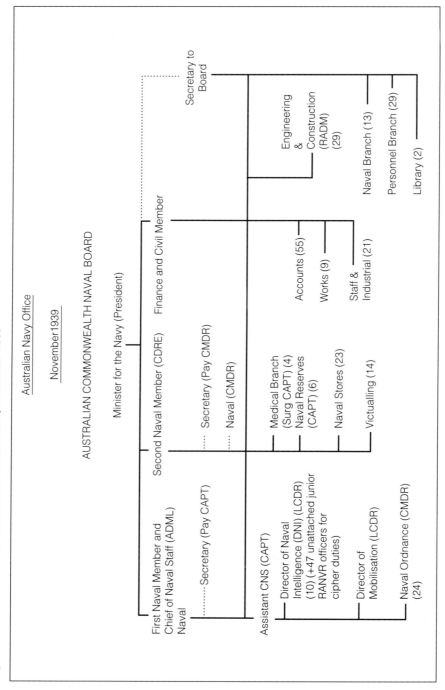

'most improbable that we would send adequate reinforcements to the Far East'.[13] The Australian naval staff, however, stuck to the proposition that 'the defection of France strengthened rather than weakened . . . recommendations for added support for Britain'.[14] The RAN's point carried and more units left for overseas service.

The key issue was to choose the moment at which the emphasis should change to regional defence. Selective appeasement of Japan seemed to have the potential to keep South-East Asia from war, while supporting the British in the Middle East would absorb the greater part of the resources available to defence. This, and Australia's very substantial technological and industrial limitations, combined to prevent any hopes of emergency naval expansion plans beyond the escort program already in progress.

The preparatory measures for a Pacific conflict that could be managed were put in place. Naval planning functioned on two levels. The first was to determine the strategy for the defence of South-East Asia, whether by British efforts centred on Malaya and Singapore, or by American intervention. The second, which most directly concerned the Australian naval staff, was the means by which effort could best be coordinated with RN forces on the China and East Indies Stations.

Attempts to clarify the strategy for the region made clear four fundamental points.

1. Australia's defence against Japan lay in Malaya and the Netherlands East Indies.
2. Britain could not be relied upon to send a main fleet to Singapore; the only outright commitment was a small force for the Indian Ocean.
3. There was no guarantee that the United States would come to the aid of the British and Dutch if the Japanese avoided attacking American possessions.
4. Perhaps most important, Britain and America were evolving a 'Germany First' strategy which carried the implication of a possible temporary abandonment of the Far East.

The British Prime Minister's assurance of August 1940 that, if finally necessary, the Mediterranean would be abandoned to provide assistance if Australia and New Zealand were actually invaded, was of little use in solving the real problems of regional defence.[15] The Australian Government certainly found it necessary to remind Britain that, whatever the Admiralty's desires, *all* Australian units would be recalled in the event of war in the Far East.[16]

Already dissatisfied with the general readiness of the British in the region[17], the RAN was insistent that some Australian ships be held back in local waters to protect merchant shipping but it took lengthy negotiations, culminating in successive visits to Singapore by Rear-Admiral J.A. Crace, the squadron commander, and Admiral Sir Ragnar Colvin (the CNS) himself before the matter was settled.[18] The dilemma of distributing inadequate forces between the defence of trade—and troop convoys—and assisting the British in the 'screen' of Malaya and the Netherlands East Indies was one that the Australian naval staff was never to resolve. Nor could it.

Phase 3: Recalling the legions

There were other difficulties. Colvin's worsening health made it apparent that he would soon require relief as CNS, while the Singapore conference of April 1941 served only to highlight differing British and American strategic concepts. It was little consolation that improved measures of cooperation with the Dutch were achieved as part of British and Australian commitments to assist with defence of the Netherlands East Indies.[19]

The middle of the year also saw the first loss of a major unit, the destroyer HMAS *Waterhen* in the Mediterranean. The British wisely refrained from claiming the scrap value to which they were entitled under terms of the ship's loan to the RAN.[20] The remaining destroyers left for Australia in June and July. *Perth*, too, came home for repairs, her place taken by HMAS *Hobart* in the last supplement to British naval forces in a distant theatre. In the meantime, Colvin had been relieved by Vice-Admiral Sir Guy Royle, formerly Fifth Sea Lord and Chief of Naval Air Services for the RN. Royle does not, however, seem to have enjoyed the confidence of the Cabinet to the same extent as Colvin[21], and the change of government in October made matters no easier.

The truth was that the Australian naval staff were only observers in the debate over the creation of an Eastern Fleet and a Far East strategy. The British were by now bankrupt in all classes of warship, part of the reason for earlier prevarication over the return of RAN ships. In the absence of air cover and sufficient escort ships, no heavy surface force could provide any kind of useful protection for Singapore. The two-phased approach eventually decided upon at Churchill's urging may have had some legitimacy as an attempt at deterrence, but its operational instructions were to prove disastrously vague.[22] Not surprisingly, anomalies in Allied strategy were still manifest in the final conference at Singapore in the first days of December, even between Australia and the United Kingdom.[23]

Phase 4: Piling Ossa on Pelion

In November 1941 HMAS *Sydney* disappeared. It was unfortunate that attempts to find survivors and evidence of her loss consumed much of the energy of the higher command in what was daily becoming a more critical strategic situation. The greatest damage done was to national morale and confidence in the Navy. News of the loss of a major ship leaked out to the public well before the Prime Minister admitted the sinking. The reputation of the ship was such that the effect of her destruction was comparable with that of HMS *Hood* on the British public earlier in the year.[24]

Sydney's loss proved to be only the first of a series of hammer blows that destroyed any remaining hope of sustaining a strategy based upon Singapore, with or without the Americans. The sinking of HM Ships *Prince of Wales* and *Repulse* spelt the end of any prospect for a useful British contribution, but the losses suffered by the United States at Pearl Harbor were the key factor. Japan could divert considerable forces to Malaya and the Netherlands East Indies without disrupting her efforts to reduce the Philippines.

By 24 December 1941, the Chiefs of Staff and the Cabinet were convinced that Singapore would fall. Just after the New Year, there came final confirmation, hardly necessary, that the RN was no longer capable of providing a battle fleet to face the Japanese.[25] Nevertheless, despite the logic behind the formation of the Australian–British–Dutch–American (ABDA) Command and, shortly afterwards, of an ANZAC area to cover Australia's north-eastern approaches, the inadequacy of the forces available forced a 'patchwork quilt' approach to Japanese thrusts which disrupted efforts to concentrate Australian naval forces in any coherent way. The poorly organised and inadequately supported ABDA naval forces suffered heavy losses. The units that did get clear to Australia enjoyed a fair measure of luck in avoiding the Japanese hunting groups in the Indian Ocean.

The RAN and the newly inaugurated Royal New Zealand Navy (RNZN) were suffering at this point from a combination of two problems. The defence of Singapore and the Dutch possessions had proved a great drain on existing strength. By numbers and types, the remaining Australian and New Zealand naval forces did not constitute the cohesive task group capable of independent offensive operations. There would be no help from other quarters. From the first, the British planned to contribute only the small carrier HMS *Hermes* to the ANZAC Force and even this decision was rapidly countermanded. While Royle's resolve, without Cabinet endorsement, not to press the Admiralty for the services of this slow and elderly ship with her small aircraft complement had some foundation of good sense, the decision had undesirable implications. Perhaps most important was that the absence of any specifically RN commitment to the ANZAC Force meant that there was no pressure on the British, moral or otherwise, to reinforce the unit, even in a token way. As a result, no major RN units were to operate with the Australian Squadron for over two years.

In addition, the need to ensure adequate American commitment dictated the appointment of a USN flag officer as Commander ANZAC Force. This did not in practice interfere with Crace, since he established his headquarters ashore, but it removed the CNS' direct responsibilities for major units on the Australia Station. Navy Office's operational role would be confined to the supervision of seaward defence and convoys.

The new arrangements were not simple to implement. The new Allied commands overlaid but did not wholly supersede the older RN station organisation under which the defence of trade was managed. The ACNB retained residual responsibilities to the Admiralty for a number of issues, in addition to the continuing requirement to confer over policy and the management of Australian manned ships under British control.

The loss of Singapore and the Netherlands East Indies meant further changes and the creation of the South Pacific and South-West Pacific Commands. This partition resulted in the separation of Australia and New Zealand, which had the consequence of separating the RNZN from the RAN except when the two Allied commands were operating in concert. This did away with an otherwise natural connection and further reduced the ability of either to achieve a critical mass for offensive operations. As a result, the hard-pressed Australian Squadron became progressively less significant in a military sense as the American naval build-up continued.

The South-West Pacific Command had other effects. The arrival of General Douglas MacArthur in Australia created a new centre of gravity for strategic decision-making. Not only Curtin and the Cabinet, but the secretary of the Department of Defence Coordination, Frederick Shedden, leant heavily on Mac-Arthur for guidance. The implications for the Australian Army have been examined at length elsewhere[26], but there were some for the RAN as well, particularly as the war drew on. MacArthur was an old rival of the USN and may have extended his attitude to cover the RAN, particularly when it appeared that the latter was pursuing independent policies.

The war with Japan made relatively little difference to most areas of technical development, apart from the production of radar. Shipbuilding was already fully extended and Australia's limited facilities came under increasing strain supporting Allied warships in both the Indian Ocean and the Pacific. The greatest priority went to strengthening the defences of the most important ports. Manpower, under heavy pressure elsewhere, was not greatly increased, beyond the commitments already in place for new construction. One valuable supplement proved to be the Women's Royal Australian Naval Service (WRANS) which was to assume much of the burden of shore administration and communications.

Phase 5: Taking up the offensive

May and June 1942 saw the successive battles of the Coral Sea and Midway and a flurry of operations by Japanese submarines in Australian waters. Despite some sinkings and disruption to trade, the offensive was limited in its effect, the Japanese not making the most of the opportunity. The achievement of the Coral Sea action in halting the Japanese advance became more obvious in the wake of the less ambiguous success at Midway; and the invasion of Guadalcanal in August signalled that the Allies had begun their own offensive. From now on, the Australian Squadron, in concert with assigned American forces, would operate as a support group for the amphibious operations in New Guinea and the South-West Pacific islands.

Not all RAN losses occurred in action with the enemy. The first loss of the war, the auxiliary minesweeper HMAS Goorangai, *collided with the coastal liner* Duntroon, *in Port Phillip Bay on 20 November 1940. She foundered immediately with the loss of her full complement of twenty-four officers and men. (AWM 128075)*

The loss of HMAS *Canberra* after the disastrous Battle of Savo in August 1942 provided a warning of how thinly stretched were expertise and personnel training.[27] Savo, however, marked the nadir of USN–RAN cooperation and integration into the American organisation became progressively smoother as time went on.

Logistic support was managed with considerable American goodwill.[28] Australian units used USN facilities except where there was specific RAN equipment involved. This inevitably meant that the major units began to carry increasing amounts of US equipment which not only ensured operational compatibility but maintained technological capabilities on more nearly equivalent levels than would have been possible with reliance on the traditional supplier. By measures such as this, the Australian forces came to form an effective and highly regarded component of the Pacific naval effort.[29] Nevertheless, there is some evidence that the Americans also viewed the Australian ships as poor relations and that the RAN became acutely aware of the much tighter financial constraints under which it operated, as well as its logistic limitations.[30]

Figure 1.2: Australian Commonwealth Naval Board, January 1945

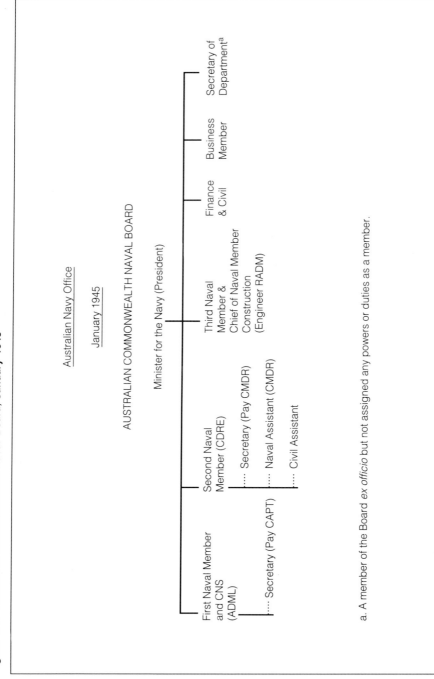

Australian Navy Office

January 1945

AUSTRALIAN COMMONWEALTH NAVAL BOARD

Minister for the Navy (President)

First Naval Member and CNS (ADML)
···· Secretary (Pay CAPT)

Second Naval Member (CDRE)
···· Secretary (Pay CMDR)
···· Naval Assistant (CMDR)
···· Civil Assistant

Third Naval Member & Chief of Naval Member Construction (Engineer RADM)

Finance & Civil

Business Member

Secretary of Department[a]

a. A member of the Board *ex officio* but not assigned any powers or duties as a member.

Nineteen forty-three saw the RAN drift to the margins of strategic decision-making. MacArthur continued to deal primarily with the Prime Minister, Sir Frederick Shedden and General Blamey, while the CNS worked with and under the Commander Naval Forces South-West Pacific. Relations at this level were good, perhaps too good for MacArthur who was suspicious of naval motives in relation to the existing command arrangements. Blamey had his own problems with MacArthur, but he also developed a jaundiced view of the RAN, which he believed to have been overly cautious in supporting the Army in New Guinea.[31] For its part, the Navy nursed suspicions that Blamey wanted to command all three services.[32]

Effort now turned towards the development of amphibious forces. The ACNB obtained approval to convert the armed merchant cruiser HMAS *Manoora* to a landing ship infantry (LSI) and similar work was soon carried out on *Westralia* and *Kanimbla*. By the middle of 1943, with the addition of American attack transports, a capable force was being developed under the designation of Amphibious Force VII. This set the theme for the next two years of largely uninterrupted progress towards Japan. The RAN's integration with the Americans ensured that it was largely unaffected by the debates over the use of Australian ground troops and the failure of MacArthur to deploy AIF units to the Philippines.

Much time was occupied in 1943 with planning for the arrival of British forces in Australia. Many of the somewhat grandiose ideas of the British 'Middle Strategy' soon proved unworkable[33], but a contribution eventually emerged in the form of the British Pacific Fleet (BPF), which began to assemble at the end of 1944.

Phase 6: Towards a post-war Navy

The prospect of the BPF and severe damage to HMAS *Hobart* after a torpedo strike highlighted the requirement for action on the future force structure. The difficulty for the RAN was that it was caught between the Government's determination to concentrate Australian activity on the war against Japan and the severe and increasing limitations on personnel and technical resources.

Royle began to think seriously on this matter some time in 1943,[34] focusing on the necessity to ensure that the RAN achieved sufficient capability to allow it to conduct operations independent of its major allies. He wrote to the First Sea Lord that the RAN required 'a Task Force of such a composition that . . . it would form such a serious threat to the enemy's line of communication that he would not be prepared to risk an overseas operation involving a large movement of troops and supplies'.[35]

Royle's efforts were two-pronged. His first approach took advantage of the decision to deploy the BPF to the Pacific. Informal discussions between Melbourne and Whitehall resulted in the offer of a light fleet carrier and two cruisers. This prospect was raised by Royle with the Advisory War Council in March 1944

Figure 1.3: Navy Office Organisation, January 1945

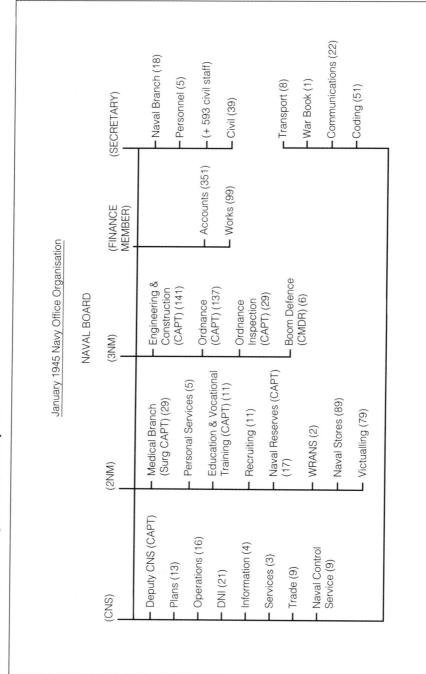

January 1945 Navy Office Organisation

NAVAL BOARD

(CNS)
- Deputy CNS (CAPT)
- Plans (13)
- Operations (16)
- DNI (21)
- Information (4)
- Services (3)
- Trade (9)
- Naval Control Service (9)

(2NM)
- Medical Branch (Surg CAPT) (29)
- Personal Services (5)
- Education & Vocational Training (CAPT) (11)
- Recruiting (11)
- Naval Reserves (CAPT) (17)
- WRANS (2)
- Naval Stores (89)
- Victualling (79)

(3NM)
- Engineering & Construction (CAPT) (141)
- Ordnance (CAPT) (137)
- Ordnance Inspection (CAPT) (29)
- Boom Defence (CMDR) (6)

(FINANCE MEMBER)
- Accounts (351)
- Works (99)

(SECRETARY)
- Naval Branch (18)
- Personnel (5)
- (+ 593 civil staff)
- Civil (39)
- Transport (8)
- War Book (1)
- Communications (22)
- Coding (51)

but met with a cold reception. There was still no relief on the issue of manpower requirements, which were now exacerbated by British requests to support the new fleet and other forces for the Pacific War.[36] Suggestions for a loan scheme, with its requirement for 4000 more men, were out of tune with the increasing emphasis on Australia's future economic wellbeing.

The plan was also caught up by the Prime Minister's justifiable irritation at the lack of response to requests made as early as October 1943 for the British to return RAN and RAAF personnel.[37] Curtin regarded the British ships as an unnecessary drain on inadequate resources and as a navy-to-navy scheme conceived without thought to overall strategic requirements. His state of mind was not improved by the discovery that Royle had been keeping the Admiralty informed of Australian War Cabinet discussions.[38]

Although the naval staff succeeded in obtaining the support of the Defence Committee for a RAN paper proposing a fleet based around at least one light fleet carrier,[39] there was opposition in unexpected quarters. Curtin still deferred to General MacArthur, who came down firmly on the side of land-based air power as the panacea for the Australian situation. Shedden was equally enthusiastic for air power and strongly objected to Royle's attempting to 'make a break ahead' of the other services.[40]

Over the following months, a bitter, albeit fragmented, debate took place between the service staffs over the size and shape of the armed forces. When agreement was finally reached, the question had then to be fought out with other consumers of manpower. Arguments related not only to future needs but wartime requirements in the light of the grave shortage of workers. The Navy's campaign had thus to be waged on two fronts.

In the short term, Royle made progress. The active role played by the Australian Squadron in the Philippines campaign strengthened his argument that the Navy required reinforcement to sustain an effective contribution. In February 1945, the Defence Committee formally recommended that the proposal go ahead, with an increase in naval recruiting to match.[41] Despite reservations, the Government finally decided to accept the loan offer. At this stage, however, the British insisted that the ships must be paid for. They were dissatisfied with the hard-nosed Australian approach to financial questions in other areas, particularly over wheat and facilities for the BPF.[42] Despite further valiant efforts by Royle to press the Navy's case, Cabinet would not agree to the expenditure of £9 000 000 for such a purpose, preferring to defer any transfer until after the war.[43] As a result, the RAN finished the conflict with only a handful of first-line combatants.

The second prong of the naval reconstruction scheme fared little better. The diminishing threat to Allied shipping put in doubt the need to continue with the entire frigate construction program, and in April of that year Cabinet agreed to cancel ten of the frigates and to meet some of the pressing requirement for amphibious transports by authorising three tank-landing ships. Royle also succeeded in obtaining approval for a cruiser and destroyer to be built in government yards. The scheme was highly attractive to the ALP for both employment and industrial development. Nevertheless, Cabinet's agreement was in principle only and the plans would be 'overwhelmed in the rising tide of victory which now made with such unexpected speed'.[44] Only the destroyer was ever built.

The more solid place of the Navy within the Government's defence plans was, however, reflected in the post-war defence policy under development. When the Prime Minister spoke in parliament on 23 March 1945, he emphasised the need for a defence system 'based on the island screen to the north' which would require conjoint 'sea-power, air-power and garrisons'. Despite the ominous note in Curtin's declaration that Australia and New Zealand were incapable of sustaining the fleet or the bases to allow them to act as bastions of Pacific defence, the general tone was encouraging.[45] The Navy could have no argument with Curtin's acknowledgment of the need for cooperation with other powers in the region; the problem would lie in determining the level of forces Australia should maintain as its contribution to such security arrangements.

The other issue that dominated naval policy in the last two years of the war was that of flag appointments. The Government remained eager to end the succession of RN loan postings to fill senior posts. Insisting that the squadron commander be Australian, Cabinet was willing to accept Collins immediately as CNS, but Royle insisted on his need for experience in command of the squadron. Curtin eventually gave way to the pleading of CNS and the Navy Minister and the Admiralty was asked to nominate a relief for Admiral Royle.[46] Both sides in this issue were right. The senior RAN candidates did need more experience before they would be fully ready for the top. On the other hand, the earlier insistence on matching Australian careers to those of the RN had left matters too late. The policy ignored the differing needs of a navy the size of the RAN which cannot afford the specialisation or the gentler pace of career development enjoyed by a large one.

The surrender of Japan found Australian ships widely scattered and under a variety of commands, reflecting the pattern of operations throughout the war. The RAN had suffered heavily during the previous six years in both men and material. Its reputation was by no means as glamorous as that which it had enjoyed in 1939. Even in the mundane but vital work of trade defence, the Australian Navy had gained few public successes. Despite over a third of its resources in men and tonnage being devoted to escort work, the RAN's ships had sunk or shared in the sinking of only seven enemy submarines.[47] In other areas, the Navy's heavy losses had been balanced by few spectacular victories and it represented to some a largely discredited and outmoded concept of defence. With the great navies of the Allies uncertain of their own future, the RAN would not find it easy to find a role and justify an existence for itself

The shortage of modern major combatants was a source of concern, but more critical were the losses of key senior officers and technical ratings and the failure to recruit for the permanent naval forces, which caused the senior naval manpower planner to suggest that the intended demands for post-war manning were 'appalling'.[48] This, even more than strategic and financial limitations, would be the key restraint on development and it was to manifest itself in more insidious ways than undermanning in the ships. The death or invaliding of several of the RAN's best prospects for senior rank must have contributed markedly to the difficulties the Navy was to encounter in the post-war era. There was simply not the intellectual capital to do all that needed to be done.

Some of the hard-learned lessons were too easily forgotten. The mine countermeasure force became very quickly moribund and would not revive until more than fifteen years later. The WRANS would go through what in retrospect was an unnecessary process of disestablishment and reactivation. Few resources were made available for the development of fleet bases other than Sydney.

There was credit in the ledger. If the RAN had generally operated as a component of greater forces, its ships had done so effectively and built up a fine reputation. For the greater part of the war, the Navy's major units had operated within Australia's area of direct strategic interest. Despite the continuing limitations of the staff and command organisation, the RAN rarely lost sight of the essential priorities for the Navy's role. The protection of sea communications had remained a key element. Some of the Navy's best work had been accomplished in support of the Army. Such interaction with land forces proved easy to resume when the Korean War began in 1951.

The RAN now had experience of working as an organisation away from the prospects of immediate support from the United Kingdom. Infrastructure had been extended and improved and the Government was conscious of the part that naval construction could play in developing domestic industrial capacity. The exposure to the RN and the USN, which many officers and sailors had enjoyed, also gave the Navy an understanding of the likely directions of future developments, which it would be prompt to exploit.

The six years had not been easy ones. The RAN, however, had achieved at least one thing in the course of the war. In 1939 there had been no doubt of the unique national identity of the Royal Australian Navy as a seagoing force, however complete its integration into the Royal Navy. What had been lacking was an appropriate independent national infrastructure to support that force. If in 1945 there remained deficiencies and some absurdities within the shore organisations and administration, there was also a much more substantial basis for the future. The RAN had at last left its childhood and entered adolescence.

2
The Pacific War: A strategic overview

Jozef H. Straczek

Throughout the first forty years of the twentieth century many books were published theorising about a possible Pacific War between Japan, Great Britain and the United States. These 'fights of fantasy' were readily taken up by audiences in all three countries. However, at the same time that authors were presenting their readers with vivid descriptions of fleet actions and troops storming the beaches, the possibility of a real Pacific War was being examined within the respective military organisations. The plans developed by Japan, Britain and America reflected the strategic, and to some extent the political, constraints under which each country expected to be operating during hostilities. This chapter describes in broad terms the pre-war strategies developed by the three Pacific powers and the strategies subsequently employed during the prosecution of the war.

Japan

In 1907 the Japanese developed their first Imperial Defence Policy, listing their potential enemies as: Russia, Germany, the United States and France. Given the limited resources of the Japanese Empire, the planners realised the difficulty of fighting a war against more than one opponent. As a consequence, Japanese diplomacy aimed at ensuring that only one enemy at a time would be faced, and that wars would be of short duration.

In response to the Imperial Defence Policy, the Imperial Japanese Navy (IJN) was given responsibility for planning a war against the US, and the IJN therefore developed a defensive strategy whereby the American Fleet would be harassed and attacked as it crossed the Pacific. Once in the western Pacific the American Fleet would be destroyed in a single decisive battle by the Japanese battle fleet. Between the conception of the defence policy in 1907 and the cessation of the Naval Arms Limitation Treaties in 1936, the basic policy underwent a number

18

hesitancy if not over-cautiousness.[11] In the wake of the Pearl Harbor disaster, US naval planning immediately returned to the 'good old days' of Stark's Plan 'Dog' Memorandum of October 1940. Plan 'Dog' had called for the major American commitment to be into the Atlantic. So despite naval reinforcement, the Pacific was seen by Stark as essentially a secondary theatre, all agreements requiring American support for Allied operations to 'divert Japanese forces away from the Malay Barrier' were cancelled. US naval forces were to be confined to an area east of 180 degrees and operations were mainly limited to protection of the Hawaii–Panama–Alaska triangle and defence of the outlying bases.[12]

In personality, Admiral King was the complete opposite of Stark—an *enfant terrible*, ebullient, aggressive, a proven risk-taker, and said by one contemporary to be 'meaner than hell'.[13] Unlike Stark, King saw the 'Europe First' orientation as a distraction, his desire was always to close with the Japanese first. US naval strategy altered accordingly. King's strategy was termed 'offensive–defensive', to 'hold what you've got and hit them when you can, the hitting to be done not only by seizing opportunities but by making them'.[14] His role was to deny the Japanese a lodgement point in the South Pacific, and he called for the occupation and fortification of the more likely air and naval base sites there, using Allied ground forces and land-based air support, while the fleet defended and launched counterstrike raids to keep the enemy off balance. From the opening rounds King wanted to make use of these bases as staging points for an early Allied counterattack.[15]

So whether one speaks of reinforcements for Fiji, Bora Bora, Canton, Christmas, Funafuti, New Caledonia, Efate or Tongatabu the hand of Admiral King was always present.[16] In the end, for all the talk of Washington's commitment to 'Germany First'—and even with the preparations in train for Operation 'Torch' (the landing in North Africa of US and Allied troops scheduled for November 1942)—the Pacific Fleet could never complain of being given short shrift in terms of resources. It had four fleet carriers to the Atlantic Fleet's one, thirteen heavy cruisers to four, 96 submarines to 28, while the two fleets were on par in light cruisers and destroyers. Though the American ground commitment to the European theatre would be greater in the long term, some 250 000 American troops were in the Pacific by late 1942, and the British were to have fair complaint regarding the relative starvation of the Atlantic in terms of merchant shipping and long-range Liberator bombers at a time when the German submarine onslaught was at its height. The USN was undoubtedly biased towards the Pacific. King's successfully fought campaign, to get 30 per cent of combined resources devoted to the war against Japan, masked a significantly higher allocation of men and *matériel* to that theatre from purely American sources. In fact they never allocated less than two-thirds of their strength in this theatre.[17]

2. Containment

Yet there were limits on the extent of the American commitment to the South

United States President Franklin D. Roosevelt and British Prime Minister Winston Churchill at the Atlantic Charter meeting aboard the battleship HMS Prince of Wales *off Newfoundland in August 1941. In the background are Admiral Ernest J. King USN (left) and the Chief of Naval Operations Admiral Harold R. Stark USN. After Pearl Harbor King became Commander-in-Chief, United States Fleet and in March 1942 he also assumed the duties of Chief of Naval Operations. (AWM 304792)*

Pacific, for the policy was by no means universally approved or accepted, and resistance came from three different directions.

When the American Army originally established the US Forces in Australia (USFIA) it had no intention of defending the continent, or of using its ground forces to create a theatre of operations. The Army regarded the Pacific as a secondary, if not a subsistence theatre, one that must not be allowed to divert vital resources from the 'real' war—the war in Europe. All the Army wanted to do—as the discussions surrounding the Pensacola convoy show—was to create a base from which to supply the Philippines. Later the Head of the Army's War Plans Division, Dwight Eisenhower, even envisaged withdrawal of US Army units once Australia's forces had been built up and her regular divisions returned from the Middle East.[18]

Rivalry between the two services was already a problem. Neither the Army nor the Navy had ever been prepared to cede to an overall commander except from their own service. The Army had consistently argued with the Navy about control of airpower over oceans, had refused to contribute manpower to the expeditionary force under War Plan 'Orange', and in 1941 would not allow Army personnel or planes to be used for garrisoning Midway, Wake and Guam. As a result, in December 1941 the Americans had four separate commands in the Pacific. Two of them—the Pacific Fleet and the Asiatic Fleet—were naval; and the other two—the Hawaiian Department and US Army Forces in the Far East—were under Army command. There was little if any coordination between them. According to one senior British observer 'the violence of interservice rivalry in the United States in these days had to be seen to be believed, and was an appreciable handicap to their war effort'.[19]

No wonder the Army was resentful of what it termed this 'creeping movement' by US forces across the Pacific. As Eisenhower wrote in February 1942:

> The Navy wants to take all the islands in the Pacific—have them held by Army troops, to become bases for Army pursuit planes and bombers. Then the Navy will have a safe place to sail its vessels.[20]

This was not far from the truth. The carving out of its own theatre of operations was a naval preoccupation. King and Nimitz had long since concluded that operations in the Pacific would be amphibious for the most part, and all amphibious operations had to come under naval control. According to MacArthur, by the end of 1942 General Marshall had become increasingly critical of what he termed 'the Navy's disregard of the common good'. Marshall felt Admiral King had:

> claimed the Pacific as the rightful domain of the Navy; he seemed to regard operations there as almost his own private war; he apparently felt that the only way to remove the blot . . . (of) the naval disaster at Pearl Harbor was to have the Navy command a great victory over Japan . . . He resented the prominent part . . . (MacArthur) had in the Pacific War; he was vehement in his personal criticism . . . and encouraged naval propaganda to that end.[21]

King's preoccupation with control meant an insistence that the main naval lines of communication extend outward from the west coast of the United States. He had little regard for Australia either as a potential base or as a springboard for operations directly north. Nothing shows the limitations concerning his desire to commit US naval forces more clearly than the following two incidents. In December 1941, at Arcadia, the British had done their best to persuade the Americans to escort convoys all the way to the Australian coast. But King had stressed each nation involved must have responsibility for a particular area, and convoying was therefore laid at the door of Australia and New Zealand for 'the USN does not wish to become deeply involved there'.[22]

Once the Australian Government knew of a proposal to establish ABDA, they expressed the greatest concern lest such a concentration of forces leave the northern and north-eastern approaches to Australia wide open to attack:

. . . no protest you make can be too strong and you should immediately seek an interview with Churchill and President to place our view before them in most emphatic manner possible. It appears to us an amazing paradox, following declaration framed to express unity of our aims and efforts that a plan should be put forward which viewed defence situation in Pacific in such a piecemeal manner.

In our opinion the plan (is) strategically unsound. The Japanese have only to avoid main allied concentrations in South West Pacific Theatre and attack (the) Australian Area which will be weakly held in order to block line of communication from America and prevent the use of Australia as a base.[23]

King directed the War Plans Division to investigate this, but they merely recommended activation of the original ABC–1 proposals for an ANZAC Area.[24] That plan called for the extension of the original operating zone to include Fiji and New Caledonia, yet Australia and New Zealand continued to be entirely responsible for naval and air patrols. The Pacific Fleet would provide escort to a prearranged and predetermined point in the ocean where ANZAC forces would take over. Fortunately Admiral Little from the British Admiralty Delegation in Washington, at the first meeting of the Combined Chiefs of Staff, was able to persuade King to make the convoy issue a matter for joint discussion between field commanders.[25]

King did try to make the ANZAC Area a US naval responsibility, first as a sub-unit of the Pacific Ocean Area and then by trying to place it under his direct and personal control. Significantly though, he believed it was essential to take steps to develop strong defences on the route to Australia and to convince the Australian Government of the need to concern itself less with its own defences and more with the protection of the lines of communications.[26] American naval reinforcement to the ANZAC Area was never more than two ships out of seventeen.[27] Australia requested the creation of a new command area—expanding the existing limits of ANZAC to include New Zealand, all the neighbouring islands as well as Timor, Ambon, all of New Guinea, and as much sea area to the west as 'might be spared'; with General Brett taking on the position of Supreme Commander, representatives from both Dominions sitting on the Combined Chiefs of Staff (CCS), and an ANZAC Council being created above the CCS. King 'hit the roof'.[28] He argued vehemently that such arrangements would 'cut across the whole system of command and operations of the United States Fleet'.[29] To his mind a more logical arrangement would be to separate Australia and New Zealand and place them in different commands—Australia and the approaches to it through New Guinea and the Dutch East Indies forming a 'strategic entity', while New Zealand belonged 'more logically with the islands along the line of communications from America'.

An enlarged ABDA Area originally proposed by the Plans Division became the boundary between SWPA and the Pacific command, now divided into three zones—North, Central and South. King spoke at length at a JCS meeting about his dissatisfaction. He accused the Australians of being too concerned with

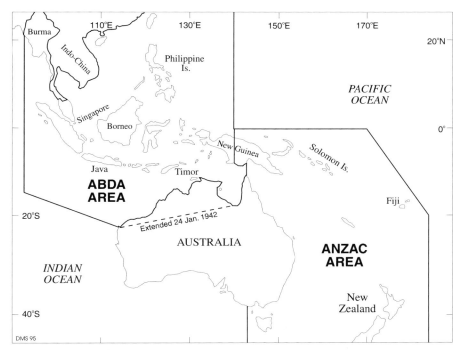

Map 3.1: *ABDA and ANZAC areas*

continental defence, and argued they had to become interested in the *approaches* to Australia. He expressed concern that Washington might 'lose control'—'it would not be possible', he said, 'for a supreme commander in Australia to control contemplated offensive operations towards the north-west. This control must be exercised from Washington'.[30] Yet he was unable to prevent the setting up of SWPA, or the name of MacArthur from being put forward as the obvious choice of supreme commander of the new area.[31] By the end of March separate South-West Pacific and Pacific Ocean Areas had been set up, one for each of the services. As the official Army history of the period has concluded:

> . . . navy planners wished to establish both areas simultaneously. Failure to do this . . . might open the way for an Army effort to enlarge the South West Pacific . . . The naval planners feared also that the Army might raise objections, if the opportunity arose, to placing forces under naval control.[32]

But, by the same token, King's policies also followed the natural path already established by US naval tradition. In their early discussions with potential allies, US planners had not seen the war as a joint effort; rather they had tried to compartmentalise, to divide and define areas of specific responsibility that each nation would control and where the rules were clearly spelled out. At ABC–1 the United States had agreed to protect American and British interests east of

39

General Douglas MacArthur, Supreme Commander Allied Forces SWPA and Australian Prime Minister, the Rt Hon. John Curtin at the Advisory War Council meeting held in Canberra 26 March 1942. They had met for the first time that day. (AWM 042774)

180 degrees, but was prepared to support Dominion naval operations south of the equator only to the Fiji Islands and as far west as 155 degrees, which included New Zealand but not Australia. US naval planners were adamant they intended to operate within their own spheres of responsibility under their own commanders. So in trying to limit US naval operations west of 155 degrees, King was simply following established policy. He had made the position abundantly clear in March 1942:

> The Pacific War is going to be an exclusive project of the Army and the Navy with as little interference as possible by outsiders. Coordination with Dutch, Australians, Chinese, New Zealanders and other allies is felt to be too unwieldy and would hamstring operations. To mollify the smaller powers a Pacific War Council was set up in Washington as a purely consultative body to allow members 'to let off steam' but not such as would in any way affect the US in its military decisions.[33]

Once the decision was taken to divide the Pacific into Army and Navy zones of control it was but a short step to the acceptance of separate axes of advance— MacArthur from the south and the Navy from the south-west. On 2 July 1942 King's prompting bore fruit. The JCS agreed to seize in sequence Tulagi and Santa Cruz, Lae, Salamaua, northern New Guinea, and finally Rabaul, and the

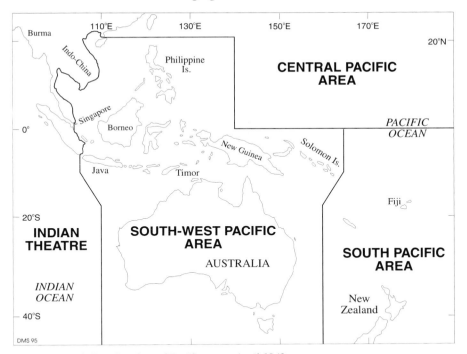

Map 3.2: *South-West Pacific and Pacific areas, April 1942*

adjacent New Guinea–New Ireland area. To ensure naval control over the operation on 1 August 1942, the boundary of SWPA was deliberately moved eastwards to place the Guadalcanal–Tulagi area originally within MacArthur's area under the control of Rear-Admiral Ghormley.

In developing his strategic ethos, King had explained to the Joint Chiefs of Staff (JCS) in March that the Fleet must fight the enemy 'where he is to be found, to seek him out rather than to husband our fighting strength at home and await his coming'. As he said, 'No fighter ever won a fight by covering up—by merely fending off the other fellow's blow. The winner hits and keeps on hitting even though he has to take some stiff blows in order to be able to keep on hitting'.[34] Such a strategy was seen by some as inordinately risky. By no means did Nimitz approve, and staff officers in the Pacific Fleet were equally unhappy about the waste in fuel and resources.[35] Yet King was adamant—'keep attacking the enemy . . . damage his ships and bases'.[36] At times the costs threatened to become exorbitantly high. USS *Lexington*, *Saratoga*, and *Enterprise* were to have raided the Gilberts in January 1942. But *Saratoga* was torpedoed and put out of action for months. Nimitz was ordered to use *Lexington* to strike at Wake, but the loss of the essential oiler forced cancellation.[37] Even at Coral Sea and Midway, where intelligence intercepts reduced the risk, two carriers were lost. King's strategy often seemed to give the appearance of 'flying by the seat of the

41

pants'. The invasion of Guadalcanal, for example, was launched with inordinate if not indecent haste. Nimitz termed it 'Operation Shoestring'.[38] Admiral Turner only took command of the amphibious forces three weeks before the landing, while the command arrangements between Ghormley, Turner and Fletcher remained loose and unspecified.[39]

Instead of a swift victory and an advance up the Solomons chain, in a series of savage naval actions around the area over the next few months the two sides battered each other into submission in a contest of wills, wildly disproportionate in terms of effort and investment for territory gained, for a singularly obscure fleck on the world's southern ocean. By mid-November 1942, American naval air power in the Pacific was dangerously vulnerable. The naval battle off Savo Island (August 8/9) had been followed by the Eastern Solomons (August 23/25), Cape Esperance (September 11/13), and the Battle of Santa Cruz (October 26/27). Each had seen 'shock and gore, exploding magazines, burning and sinking ships and plummeting planes—that is simply how it was'.[40] USS *Wasp* and *Hornet* had been sunk while *Saratoga* was again badly damaged. By mid-September only *Enterprise* was still in combat. America had been reduced to one carrier in the Pacific, and it would eventually take six months and 3000 Australian and American lives before the area was secured for Allied forces.

This helps explain the third element of resistance to King's program, for it was understandable under such circumstances that the USN should return to the familiar past to solve the perceived impasse. During the inter-war period American war plans were colour coded—war against Germany was 'Black', against Mexico 'Green' and Britain 'Red'. War against Japan had been deemed 'Orange'. War Plan 'Orange'—initiated in 1907—had called for a trans-Pacific offensive, primarily naval in character but with a military expeditionary force in tow, to the rescue and relief of America's primary Far Eastern possession, the Philippines. Once rescue had taken place the Fleet would proceed to harass, isolate and blockade the Japanese home islands.[41] At the centre of the plan was the presumption that the Army could hold out until the Navy arrived to the rescue.

As the inter-war period proceeded the period before relief—like that of Britain's Singapore strategy—became longer and longer.[42] By 1938 it was expected the Navy would have to seize the Marshalls and the Carolines and perhaps all of the Mandates first. They provided no timetable for rescue. But the Navy never gave up on War Plan 'Orange'. On 16 April 1942 Rear-Admiral Kelly Turner urged the Navy to consider launching a completely new Central Pacific drive into the Marshalls and the Carolines.[43] But King himself had mentioned the possibility of operating to the north-west of the Mandates as early as 21 January.[44] However, it was not until the last day of November 1942 that King finally baulked at continuing the frontal assault up the Solomons chain, suggesting outflanking operations further north to Marshall and Nimitz.[45] By 9 February 1943 King was calling for an advance from Midway to the Truk–Guam line.[46] The Navy War Plans Division responded that the Gilberts were an option. The islands had the advantage that they were within the range of land-based aviation support. The reaction of the Pacific Fleet was effusive.[47] By the middle of the year the American Navy had returned to the traditional values of War Plan 'Orange' and between March and September 1943 King and the Navy succeeded in convincing the JCS to open a third axis of advance.

The surest way to defeat Japan was with maximum efficiency. That meant applying maximum force under a supreme command along the shortest route. It was quicker to reach Manila via the northern axis, where the land masses offered opportunities to establish air bases in considerable numbers with better cost savings than the vast sprawl of islands in the Mandates. Australia then was the most obvious springboard along that axis, and the only practicable advanced base—one that had already been established. In the end American naval conduct of the Pacific war was to prove wasteful both in terms of the allocation of resources, and in dispersion of effort. The USN consistently failed to pursue the most efficient and economic strategy against the Japanese. As General Arnold wrote:

> . . . throughout the war we continued operating in our inefficient way, with first three, then two commands . . . both working towards the same end—the defeat of Japan, with overlapping lines of communications, overlapping air operations, overlapping sea operations, and finally, overlapping land Army operations. In my opinion that was one hell of a way to run a war.[48]

4
The effect of World War II on RAN–RN relations

Alastair Cooper

The dominant influence on the Royal Australian Navy, from before its creation in 1911 until the start of the Pacific War in 1941, was Britain's Royal Navy. The Pacific War marked the start of a gradual reduction in that influence, though it is still evident in the RAN today. After the war the relationship was different in its character and underwent enormous changes over the next two and a half decades. This makes the wartime relationship between the two navies particularly noteworthy, as the changes wrought were the origin of a fundamental shift in relations between them in the period from 1945 to 1971. This chapter discusses some aspects of that relationship which exemplify its character; the planning for the shape of the post-war RAN, tactical signalling and the exchanges and loans of personnel between the two navies.

Planning the post-war fleet

In 1911 the Minister for Defence, Senator George Pearce, described the RAN as 'a navy within a navy', a description that was still accurate in 1939.[1] The RAN entered World War II with a fleet based on two heavy cruisers, four light cruisers and five destroyers. All were RN designs and with the exception of the oldest cruiser, HMAS *Adelaide*, all were built in Britain. They were in almost every aspect the same as their RN counterparts; built to the same designs by the same shipyards, modified and maintained on similar scales.[2] While this convention was maintained when practical during the war it was not alway possible. One example where it was not possible was the Type 271 radar, the first centimetric radar widely operated by the RN.[3] Mainly as a result of unhindered access to US and British technology Australia was able to design and produce its own version. The A271A radar operated on slightly longer wavelengths than the original set but was still suitable for the *Bathurst* class minesweepers built in Australia during the war. This is but one example of the way in which the demands of the war, in this case on shipping and production, changed the RAN's supply situation and, as a result, its relationship with the RN.[4] Other examples include Australia's armaments industry, which developed the capacity to manufacture many types of naval ordnance. The requirement for large numbers of escort vessels led to a revival in the Australian shipbuilding industry, which supplied ships to the Royal and Indian Navies as well as the RAN.[5] Three Tribal class destroyers, twelve River and Bay class frigates, sixty minesweepers and other smaller craft were built during the war. These examples of Australia's self-sufficiency are significant because they reduced the RAN's dependence upon the RN and by the end of World War II the RAN was independent in some areas of equipment acquisition.[6]

While wartime constraints did lead to greater self-sufficiency in the Australian Navy, they did not by any means lead to an abandonment of Britain as a source of ships. When in 1944 the ACNB started to consider the shape of Australia's post-war Navy, it hoped to acquire aircraft carriers, cruisers and destroyers from Britain.[7] As the RN had more ships in commission and building than it could maintain after the war, it was extremely keen for some to be transferred to friendly navies in and outside the Commonwealth.[8] The British Government had a number of reasons for approving the sale. It would increase the Commonwealth's defences, spread the financial burden of that defence, and above all reduce British war debts. In Australia's case the sale could be offset against the debt incurred by the BPF's basing in Australia.[9] The Australian Government for its part was keen to recover as much of the debt as possible, and was wary of any attempt by the British Treasury to pay it out by increasing the price of the ships.[10]

The transfer of cruisers did not eventuate, but it does illustrate the way in which Anglo–Australian naval relations were very closely linked to the political climate of the day. Both the Admiralty and the ACNB were well aware of the Australian Government's suspicion that the RAN's close links with the RN would result in Australia's acquiring inferior and/or exorbitantly priced ships.[11] Though Australian political caution may have slowed the acquisition process it was definitely not a complete rejection of the RN's assistance.[12] In contrast to the inter-war years, the benefits of the RAN–RN relationship were not taken to be axiomatic, and the Naval Board and Admiralty had to demonstrate its advantages.

Foremost among the RAN's post-war plans for the make-up of the fleet was the acquisition of two aircraft carriers. The issues surrounding the three carriers that served in Australia's Navy were for the next fifteen years central to the RAN's relationship with the RN. Both in terms of capabilities, equipment and personnel they were the RAN's most significant and complicated assets. As a result they were the basis for much of the RAN's claim for a voice in strategic planning in the South-East Asian region.

The main issue that arose, after whether or not the RAN should acquire aircraft carriers, was how much Australia was willing to pay for them.[13] Both were political decisions and there was not much enthusiasm in the Australian Government for '. . . (spending) £9 000 000 on ships built in another country',

The flotilla leader HMAS Stuart *with the Mediterranean Fleet in 1940. After returning to Australia she was first modified for the role of escort destroyer and later for duty as a fast troop transport.* Stuart *survived the war and was paid off in 1946. (AWM 128070)*

even though they were being offered at a reduced price.[14] In the end it was not until after the war that the government accepted the RAN's plan to acquire two carriers built in Britain, starting almost forty years of carrier operations. The issue, however, was never completely settled, mainly because operating two carriers was at the extremities of the RAN's financial and manning capabilities, and also because of questions arising from delays in completing and modernising the carriers. If anything, the establishment of a naval air arm in Australia strengthened ties between the RN and the RAN. Not only did the RAN use the promise of RN assistance to thwart the RAAF in their attempts to gain control over naval aviation, but it also relied upon the RN to assist with the initial manning as well as to train Australian personnel.[15]

From the RAN's perspective it was understood that, although the new carriers were to be built in Britain, there was a political as well as strategic requirement for the maintenance of an Australian shipbuilding industry. The ACNB proposed a building program of destroyers and accepted the Australian consensus that all ships of destroyer size and below were to be built locally, though still to RN designs.[16] In the interim, five 'Q' class destroyers were transferred from the RN to cover the period until ships from the RAN's building program could be brought into service.[17] The effects of the decision to build destroyers for the RAN in Australia held significant implications for its relationship with the RN. In particular it brought Australia's Navy closer to the design and building process,

gloom deepened as his fleet was reduced to service the war against Germany. This had the positive effect, however, of providing the context for the first major deployment of Australian naval assets to the area. In September 1939 the Admiralty and ACNB had agreed to deploy Australia's destroyer force (on loan from the UK since 1933) for service outside the Australian station. These ships, the *Scott* class leader HMAS *Stuart* and 'V/W' class destroyers HMA Ships *Vampire*, *Vendetta*, *Voyager* and *Waterhen*, were on passage to Singapore for training when a signal was received from the Admiralty on 16 October asking for their services to help replace the 8th Flotilla in the Mediterranean. On 21 October Pound was informed by Admiral Colvin, First Naval Member, that 'the Australian Government would definitely not wish to impede any dispositions regarded as essential'.[3] Such an important decision could not, however, be settled between the two officers and it had to be decided at government level. On the promise of the dispatch of some old light cruisers for trade defence (which never actually appeared) the move of the destroyers was approved by the Australian Cabinet on the last day of October and the Admiralty was so informed on 4 November. The British promised the ships would be returned or replaced by suitable similar units in Australian waters if a submarine threat appeared there. Under the command of Commander H.M.L. Waller RAN, the five Australian ships sailed from Singapore on 13 November, the day before the formal Dominions Office request for their transfer reached the Australian Government! They were at Malta by Christmas after some of the group had been diverted in the Indian Ocean to join in the hunt for the *Graf Spee*.

Immortalised later as the 'Scrap Iron Flotilla' the Australian ships were all over twenty-years old. Only *Stuart* was up to modern standards of destroyer armament with 4.7-inch guns; the 'V/W's only had 4-inch weapons. What they lacked in firepower they made up for in the quality of their crews, who Cunningham characterised as 'the most lively and undefeated fellows I have ever had to do with'—high praise indeed from such a source.[4] As the 19th Destroyer Division, their main role was to act as escorts and patrols throughout the Mediterranean area. In mid-winter they formed the main strength of the depleted fleet but reinforcements appeared as 1940 wore on and in late May the Australian ships were combined with the four, more modern British 'D' class destroyers of the 20th Division to form the 10th Destroyer Flotilla with Waller as Captain (D). When war with Italy came two weeks later, the Australian destroyers provided five out of the twenty-two destroyers on station in the Mediterranean Fleet. Cunningham, or rather Admiral Tovey, Vice-Admiral Light Forces, also had five modern light cruisers, one of which was HMAS *Sydney* which had arrived at Alexandria through the Suez Canal on 26 May under the command of Captain John Collins to join the 7th Cruiser Squadron. It had been intended originally that *Sydney* should be deployed in the Red Sea but Cunningham told Collins that he had been so impressed with Waller's ships that he had decided to keep the Australian cruiser for himself.[5]

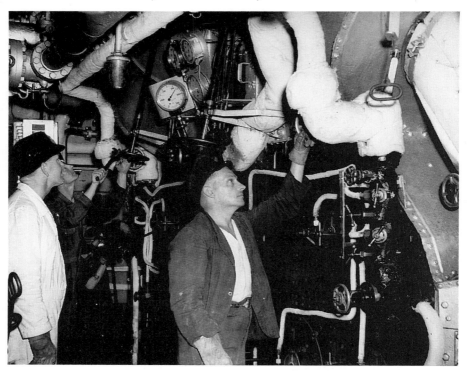

The forward boiler room of the modified Leander *class cruiser HMAS* Sydney. *Under Captain John Collins,* Sydney *won fame for her actions against the Italians in the Mediterranean in 1940. Returning to Australian waters in February 1941* Sydney *was employed as a convoy escort until 19 November 1941, when she was lost with all hands in action with the German raider* Kormoran. *(AWM 5714)*

In the first days of the war *Sydney* took part in Cunningham's inaugural sweep into the eastern Mediterranean, while the 10th Flotilla destroyers returned to contest the approaches to Alexandria with Italian mine-laying submarines. Waller's flotilla was able to scout a channel through which the fleet could return to base. *Sydney* and *Stuart* also participated in an Anglo–French bombardment of Bardia on the night of 20–21 June. This was the last time the Allies operated together as France signed an armistice on 22 June.

The first significant surface action of the Mediterranean war ensued on 28 June when the 7th Cruiser Squadron, supporting two Malta–Alexandria convoys, was directed by aircraft to three large Italian destroyers carrying troops to Libya. One of the destroyers, *Espero*, was disabled and finished off by *Sydney*, but in the difficult chase conditions in failing light the cruisers fired off most of their ammunition and the Malta convoys had to be postponed. *Vampire*, however, formed part of the escort of a convoy to Alexandria from the Aegean that was successfully run. *Voyager* was also involved in an offensive anti-submarine sweep by five destroyers that resulted in the sinking of two Italian submarines. In a subsequent hunt based on intelligence gleaned from survivors, *Stuart* and HMS *Hostile* attacked a third submarine but without result.

The postponed convoys from Malta carrying evacuees and fleet stores sailed on 9 July, covered by almost the entire fleet that had sailed from Alexandria two days before. *Stuart* was operating with the cruisers supported by the faster battleship HMS *Warspite*, and *Vampire* and *Voyager* were escorting the slower component of the battlefleet, the battleships HMS *Malaya* and HMS *Royal Sovereign* and the carrier HMS *Eagle*. A powerful Italian force of two battleships was spotted by air reconnaissance moving northwards and Cunningham sailed to cut off the enemy from home. Before action was joined *Stuart* was redeployed to escort the slower battleships while the two Australian 'V/W's escorted *Eagle* as she manoeuvred for flying operations. Together with the British cruisers, *Sydney* was hotly engaged in a long-range action with heavier Italian ships which had the advantage of the light. *Warspite* joined in and was able to score a hit on the Italian battleship *Giulio Cesare* at extreme range. This caused the Italians to break off the action. *Stuart* was involved in the subsequent destroyer fighting as the Italians tried to cover their retreat; *Sydney* also gave useful support to the flotillas. The battle off Calabria demonstrated to the Italians the greater gunnery abilities of the British fleet and confirmed its moral superiority. The convoys got through this time, escorted by forces that included the Australian destroyers. The Italians attacked from the air to no great effect, although *Vampire* suffered the first RAN death-in-action of the war when she was straddled by bombs.[6] *Sydney* had fired off all her AA ammunition before she returned to Alexandria.[7]

Italian woes continued on 19 July when *Sydney*, providing support for anti-submarine destroyer operations north of Crete, engaged two more lightly protected but equally armed Italian cruisers on passage from Tripoli to Leros. The encounter was in part fortuitous as Collins had decided to stay with the destroyers after passing through the Kaso Strait rather than making northwards in search of enemy shipping as originally intended.[8] Italian fire proved ineffective but, despite the lack of an aircraft to spot for her guns, *Sydney*, an experienced gunnery ship by this time (by the end of the action she had fired 2200 main armament rounds in two weeks) had little difficulty in hitting both enemy ships.[9] One, *Giovanni Delle Bande Nere*, was able to get away but the other, *Bartolomeo Colleoni*, was devastated, to be finished off by two of the destroyers. The action off Cape Spada was a classic cruiser engagement and Collins and his ship deserved their rapturous welcome back at Alexandria, the Australian destroyers showing particular enthusiasm and no less than 35 Australian flags.

Before the end of July the Mediterranean fleet was yet again at sea covering Aegean convoys and trying to intercept a Greek ship carrying fuel to the Dodecanese. *Sydney* and HMS *Neptune* found and destroyed the latter while Australian destroyers formed part of the escort and carried out diversionary operations to distract the Italians. Cunningham had proved that, despite numerically inferior forces, he could engage in successful sea control operations in the eastern Mediterranean. In September he turned his attention to trying power projection. In mid-August the 10th Flotilla supported a major bombardment of Capuzzo while a week later Waller, covered by Collins, led an attack with destroyers on the seaplane base in the Gulf of Bomba. Simultaneously the gunboat *Ladybird* covered by *Waterhen* attacked Bardia.

At the beginning of September 1940 the Mediterranean Fleet received significant reinforcement. The modernised HMS *Valiant* replaced *Royal Sovereign* and HMS *Illustrious* supplemented *Eagle*. As part of the operation to bring in the new ships from the western Mediterranean, *Sydney*, disguised as an Italian cruiser, bombarded the Makri Yalo airfield at the south end of Scarpanto. The operations of the preceding weeks were taking their toll on all ships, not least on the old Australian destroyers, two of which were in dockyard hands for at least part of September. When at the end of the month the fleet sailed to cover a troop convoy to Malta, only *Stuart* was with it and she was on her way to refit there. After picking up a downed Fulmar pilot however, her steam piping finally gave way and she had to return to Alexandria. In the event this was a stroke of luck, for the old destroyer leader, commanded by her Navigating Officer, Lieutenant-Commander N.J.M. Teacher RN, found the Italian submarine *Gondar* attempting a *Miale* human torpedo attack on Alexandria. After a copybook asdic hunt the boat was forced to the surface and scuttled herself. After another Malta convoy operation both *Stuart* and *Vendetta* refitted in the dockyard there, the Italian air threat having proved not as serious as had been expected before the war. While supporting this convoy *Sydney* was involved in the cruiser operations that sank the destroyer *Artigliere*.

At the end of October, *Voyager* and *Vampire* accompanied the 'slow' second division of the Fleet to cover an Aegean convoy and mount an air strike on Maltezana in the Dodecanese, while *Sydney* penetrated as far as the Dardanelles as part of a cruiser–destroyer surface action group (SAG) exercising contraband control in the Aegean. The Italian invasion of Greece now allowed the establishment of a base at Suda Bay. *Vampire*, *Voyager* and *Waterhen* provided the escort for the first Crete convoy covered by *Sydney* and the rest of the Fleet.

The Australian ships were also involved in the complex of operations associated with the Taranto raid in November 1940. The V/Ws escorted convoys while *Sydney* acted as a high-speed troop transport for Suda Bay before joining the main body of the Fleet for a supplementary cruiser–destroyer raid into the Adriatic. *Sydney*, *Ajax*, *Nubian* and *Mohawk* formed a powerful SAG which found and destroyed a four-ship convoy.

After Taranto had neutralised the Italian surface fleet, Cunningham was able to exploit sea communications between Alexandria, Malta, Greece and Crete with little fear of interdiction. The Mediterranean line of communication was even reopened for important cargoes, and carrier air strikes were carried out on the Dodecanese and Tripoli. *Sydney* and the Australian destroyers played a full part in these operations, the cruiser sailing 2628 miles in one week at the end of November.[10] At the beginning of 1941, after a visit to Malta for repairs, the hard-worked cruiser was ordered home. Unknown to Collins and his ship's company, the ACNB had decided on 9 December that they needed more of their assets in home waters to cope with the raider threat. It was decided, however, to relieve *Sydney* by her sister, HMAS *Perth*, and the latter arrived at Alexandria on Christmas Eve.[11]

In December 1940 O'Connor's counterattack in the Western Desert began and the Italian army in North Africa was smashed. Cunningham formed an Inshore Squadron to support the army composed of the monitor HMS *Terror* and the river gunboats *Aphis* and *Ladybird*, supported by the Australian destroyers. It made sense to use these latter assets in this littoral role given their combination of limited technical capabilities and considerable fighting spirit. Waller, in whom Cunningham had the highest confidence, was made Senior Officer Afloat for operations in support of the Army. Minesweepers and anti-submarine trawlers were also allocated to him. The Inshore Squadron patrolled offensively along the coast, bombarded, protected supply vessels and water carriers, and 'generally maintained the essential sea supply lines to the rapidly moving battle front'.[12] The destroyers were able to add captured Italian guns to their AA armament, which was steadily enhanced to deal with the air threat, low-angle guns or torpedo tubes being deleted to compensate.[13] The Inshore Squadron assisted in the capture of Bardia at the beginning of 1941. On *Stuart's* return to service on 10 January, Waller reverted to being Captain (D) of the 10th Flotilla for more general service but he and his Australian ships were back with the Inshore Squadron to support the taking of Tobruk by the Sixth Australian Division on 22 January. Wavell stressed the importance of a strong seaward flank in his dispatch on the campaign:

> The maintenance problem in this quick moving operation over a distance of 500 miles would have been insurmountable without the Navy's assistance in keeping open the supply lines and opening up of Salum, Bardia and Tobruk, thereby shortening lines of communication and releasing motor transport for the vital task of stocking up successive field supply depots.[14]

Cunningham's own high opinion of Waller was shown on 7 February when Prime Minister Menzies was being shown round the fleet at Alexandria. As the ministerial party approached *Stuart*, the CinC remarked, 'And now you are going to meet one of the greatest captains who ever sailed the seas—his name is Waller.'[15]

Up to now the Mediterranean campaign had been a useful use of the restricted assets of the British Empire. The Mediterranean had been at least partially reopened and morale-boosting defeats inflicted on at least one enemy. Now it was all to change. Hitler was forced to come to his hapless ally's rescue with both ground forces and powerful anti-shipping air power. British strategic errors compounded the problems. The decision to reinforce Greece against possible German attack prevented the consummation of the North African campaign. Opposition off the North African littoral became more serious and the 10th

Flotilla was largely diverted to escorting convoys to Greece. By the time the Australian ships returned to littoral duties at the beginning of April, withdrawal from the gains of the previous months was in full swing. Tobruk and its Australian garrison was invested by 10 April and the Inshore Squadron did what it could to bombard the enemy positions and maintain maritime communications with Tobruk in the face of effective Axis air attacks.

Before the end of January the German air threat had reversed the strategic situation in the central Mediterranean. While covering the 'Excess' convoy, and screened by *Perth* among others, *Illustrious* was crippled by German dive-bombers. She was repaired under heavy air attack at Malta, alongside *Perth* forced to put in for boiler repairs. With Malta's first 'air siege' thus begun, this was a race between the repair parties and the *Luftwaffe*. *Perth* helped put out fires in the carrier before escaping to Alexandria on 18 January. She was next engaged in 'Lustre', the movement of troops to Greece, taking the role of troopship herself. When the Germans persuaded the Italians to try to interdict this flow with a major fleet operation the stage was set for the largest fleet engagement of the Mediterranean war.

This is not the place to go into the details of the Battle of Cape Matapan (28–29 March 1941).[16] *Perth* formed part of Pridham-Wippell's cruiser force, while Waller led two 'G' and two 'H' class destroyers in *Stuart* (the 'V/W's were not really up to fleet duties by this time; *Vendetta* escorting the cruisers developed engine trouble and had to return to Alexandria). *Stuart* played an exciting if confusing role in the night action with both guns and torpedoes. Her Italian light armament acted as useful cover. The events of that night are perhaps best summed up by the CinC:

> . . . the movements and results achieved by HMAS *Stuart*'s division during the night must remain obscure. HMS *Havock* certainly sank an enemy destroyer, they had an exciting night and did considerable execution, but the presence of undamaged enemy cruisers in the area at the time seems unlikely and it is not improbable that the ships so reported by HMAS *Stuart* were in fact some of the others of his own division.[17]

In the event both the destroyers *Alfieri* and *Carducci* were sunk by Waller's ships but two others escaped. James Goldrick's assessment seems a fair one: 'Given the British and Australian destroyer crews' inexperience in night fighting, which forced them to operate independently rather than as a coordinated unit, and the Italians' superior speed, such results were probably as good as could be expected.'[18] *Stuart* had a large number of recent drafts on board whom Waller praised for their good work. With the loss of three heavy cruisers, and the narrow escape of a damaged battleship, the Italians were again deterred from interfering in subsequent operations, despite the successes of German air power and ground forces.

The reinforcement of Greece turned into evacuation—'Operation Demon'—at the end of April as the Germans struck and carried all before them. The Australian ships played a full part, both as convoy escorts and as evacuation assets

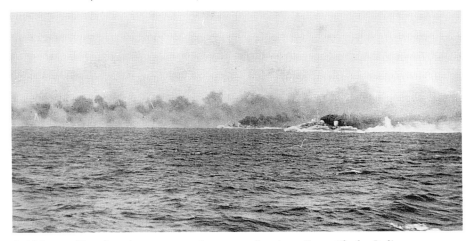

British warships throwing out a smokescreen when in action with the Italian battleship Vittoria Veneto *during the Battle of Matapan on 28 March 1941. The cruiser HMAS* Perth *is in the foreground.* Perth *was sunk on 1 March 1942 in company with USS* Houston *while courageously engaging a vastly superior Japanese force taking part in the invasion of Java. (AWM 7044)*

themselves. The operation went as well as could be expected except for the unfortunate affair off Kalamata where Bowyer Smith, *Perth*'s RN captain, decided that withdrawing the 7000 troops there was unduly risky, given the importance of the remaining light forces forming Force 'B' under his command (two cruisers and nine destroyers) to the residual strength of the Mediterranean Fleet. Over-cautiously he considered the threat of Italian surface attack to be too serious with his ships silhouetted against the fires ashore. Cunningham characterised his decision as 'unfortunate' and it is difficult not to agree given the clear evidence by that time of Italian lack of capacity for night surface action.[19]

Before the Germans moved on to Crete two more RAN destroyers arrived in the Mediterranean. The Australian ships' companies of the destroyer division in the Mediterranean had so impressed Cunningham and Tovey that they had recommended in April 1940 that they be sent to the UK to commission five powerful new ships. The plans were disrupted by Italy's entry into the war but new Australian drafts, many of them Naval Reserves, were sent to the UK to man the five new 'N' class destroyers earmarked for loan to the RAN. The first two, HMA Ships *Napier* and *Nizam*, were duly commissioned in November–December 1940 and both arrived in the Mediterranean in early May 1941. Waller was the only qualified Captain (D) in the RAN and the flotilla had to be commanded by Captain S.H.T. Arliss RN as Captain (D) 7th Flotilla.[20]

The older Australian ships helped escort convoys to and from Crete in May and the newer ships along with the cruiser *Perth* operated with the main Fleet covering the island. *Perth* assisted in the massacre of the seaborne component of the German invasion forces, but the Fleet could do little to prevent the airborne landings. *Stuart* and *Nizam* were involved in the attempts to reinforce Crete, while *Voyager* and *Vendetta* helped escort *Formidable* in the raid on the Scarpanto airfield. When evacuation proved necessary the whole Mediterranean Fleet was strained to the utmost to get the troops off under the heavy assault from the air. *Perth* embarked landing craft to evacuate troops from Sfakia and had her forward boiler room put out of action by a bomb on the way back to Alexandria. The two 'N's were involved in completing the Sfakia evacuation, an operation ably supervised by the beachmaster Lieutenant L.M. Hinchliffe RAN. On the run to Alexandria, *Napier* was near-missed by a bomb and forced to a standstill, her engine room parties getting her underway again after half an hour. The Australian ships were fortunate not to suffer more greatly in a series of actions that cost the Mediterranean Fleet three cruisers and six destroyers sunk and two battle-ships, a carrier, two cruisers and two destroyers seriously damaged. Both Australian 'N's needed repairs. The 'Scrap Iron Flotilla' also suffered a loss when, after avoiding damage off Crete and surviving two last Tobruk runs, *Vampire* was forced to sail for Singapore on 28 May, her machinery trouble having become terminal.

Now perhaps was the time for a major strategic revision. The Mediterranean had become a 'black hole' sucking in precious forces that could have been of greater use elsewhere. Even before the Crete debacle Curtin, the Australian opposition leader, had spoken basic good sense in the Advisory War Council on 8 May when he suggested the vacation of the Mediterranean and the deployment of Australian assets closer to home.[21] Only the day before, however, Churchill had forced on the Chiefs of Staff the political assumption that Japan was not going to enter the war so there was no need to reinforce further the Far East and sustain the pre-war priority for Singapore.[22] The majority of the War Council seems to have echoed Churchill's view and Menzies had little difficulty in overruling Curtin when the latter repeated his suggestion for a strategic reassess-ment. Sadly the Labor leader had combined his idea of closing the Suez Canal and holding Palestine with an ill-considered suggested withdrawal from all of Africa. This gave an all too easy target for Menzies and allowed the Prime Minister to uphold the Mediterranean priority.

So, as Japan began to move towards war, the Imperial forces that might have deterred or prevented her, and which had been intended pre-war to do just that, remained deployed elsewhere, for little overall strategic return. One of their more useful tasks was littoral support for the conquest of Syria, with *Perth*, *Stuart* and *Nizam* assisting in bombardments. Several French batteries were destroyed by *Perth's* accurate fire. The sloop HMAS *Parramatta*, in the Mediterranean since 3 June, also escorted reinforcements to Cyprus.

The main duty of the older Australian destroyers was in maintaining the Tobruk Ferry Service to the Australian garrison at the isolated town. A regular warship shuttle service for troops, ammunition and stores ran from early May

1941. By mid-June all four of the remaining Australian 'V/W's were engaged in this duty. Some 139 runs were made, 39 of them by *Vendetta* which carried 1552 troops into Tobruk, 2951 away (including wounded and POWs) and 616 tons of supplies in.[23] This process finally wore out the 'Scrap Iron Flotilla'; first *Voyager* and then *Stuart* were sent for refit while poor *Waterhen* was dive-bombed and sunk on 29 June, the first RAN loss to enemy action. Cunningham visited *Stuart* on the day she sailed for Australia on 22 August to express personally his gratitude for what she and the rest of her flotilla had done. He paid special tribute to 'the Black Squad' who had 'done magnificently to keep these ships going'.[24]

Vendetta passed to the 7th Flotilla until she too sailed east, bound for Singapore in October, having been employed in convoy work following her last Tobruk run on 3 August. The two Australian 'N's took their turn on Tobruk duties in August and September while *Parramatta* escorted slow merchantmen to and from the port. The first Australian minesweeper–corvette, HMAS *Bathurst*, also arrived in the Mediterranean in August but was sent back to the Red Sea because of her lack of AA armament.

Perth was replaced by HMAS *Hobart* in July while that month a third RAN 'N', HMAS *Nestor*, took part in operation 'Substance' to supply Malta from the west. *Nestor* distinguished herself in evacuating the troops from a torpedoed merchantman and survived the fierce Axis assaults that sank another destroyer and damaged a cruiser. With the withdrawal of the *Luftwaffe* to Russia, Malta was in the process of being built up into a useful offensive base, a role in which she briefly served in late 1941. In September and October 1941 *Hobart* and the two Australian 'N's took part in the intensive operations to withdraw the Sixth Australian Division from Tobruk and replace it with the British 70th Division. Australian insistence on this move caused a lot of ill feeling in London—not least from Churchill. Its political advisability was indeed questionable but at least Australian ships shared the risks of the hazardous movement.[25]

On 18 November the 'Crusader' offensive began in the desert and this required supplying the Tobruk garrison so it could play its part. There were now two RAN sloops available for escort duty, HMAS *Yarra* having arrived on 14 November. Both ships escorted a convoy on the day 'Crusader' opened and then on 25 November, *Parramatta* together with a British *Hunt* class escort destroyer took an ammunition ship westwards. In the early hours of 27 November *Parramatta* was sunk by a torpedo fired by *U 599*, one of the recently deployed German submarines that were having a very good month indeed. She was not the major loss of that period but it was only fitting that Australia should share in the disasters that overtook both Somerville and Cunningham at this time. By 20 December the Mediterranean Fleet and Force 'H' as they existed for the previous year had disappeared thanks to U-boats, mines, and *Miale* human torpedoes.

Napier and *Nizam* were escorting the battleship HMS *Barham* when she was sunk spectacularly by *U 331* on 25 November. *Nizam* helped pick up the

The 'N' class destroyer HMAS Norman, *one of five transferred to the RAN in 1940–41. After service in the Mediterranean the four surviving destroyers served in the Indian and Pacific Oceans until the end of the war. They paid off and reverted to the RN in October 1945. (RAN)*

450 survivors. The two ships then took part in an abortive operation to intercept a supposed Italian force in the Ionian Sea. *Napier* had to dock for repairs leaving *Nizam* to form part of the escort to the fast supply ship *Breconshire* on a Malta run. This led to the first battle of Sirte when Admiral Vian successfully drew off a powerful Italian surface force, including two battleships. After her operations with the Gibraltar-based Force 'H', *Nestor* briefly joined Cunningham with the escort of a convoy from Malta on 29 December. She carried out a bombardment of Bardia with *Napier* and *Nizam* on New Year's Eve, but for understandable reasons the three Australian ships left to fight Japan on 3 January 1942. *Hobart* and *Yarra* had already gone, the former on 9 December—the date the official request for their withdrawal was received (another case of Admiralty 'mind-reading')—and the latter on 16 December. *Hobart* had ended her duties with Cunningham with a bombardment in support of the land campaign and an uneventful covering operation for *Breconshire* from Malta. *Yarra* had escorted a last Tobruk convoy during which she towed the damaged British sloop *Flamingo* into Tobruk after the latter had been near-missed and crippled by air attack.

Many of the ships that had survived in the Mediterranean were to be sunk by the Japanese in the opening months of 1942. Whether their earlier deployment in stronger, more coherent forces would have saved them is a matter for discussion. Following the retreat of the Eastern Fleet across the Indian Ocean after the Colombo raid in April, its four Australian 'N's—*Norman, Nizam, Napier* and *Nestor*—were sent to the Mediterranean to be drawn into the operations to sustain 'the Verdun of Maritime War', Malta.[26] By this time the North African campaign was being fought for Malta rather than vice versa, the only justification, perhaps, being the loss of prestige the fall of yet another Imperial 'fortress' might be. Supplying Malta, however, was a disproportionately expensive business, given the return of the *Luftwaffe* to the Mediterranean in strength. During Operation 'Vigorous', *Nestor* was straddled by two bombs and mortally damaged.[27] She had to be sunk on 16 June by HMS *Javelin* that had been attempting to tow her back to Alexandria. The remaining three 'N's returned to the Indian Ocean.

The next Australian destroyer to see Mediterranean service was during the 'Torch' operations in November. The new fleet destroyer HMAS *Quiberon* formed part of the cruiser–destroyer SAG Force 'Q' tasked with interdicting sea communications between Bizerta and Tunis. *Quiberon* shared in the destruction of an Italian submarine and that of an entire convoy of four ships and escort. She later removed the crew of her sister HMS *Quentin* when the latter was sunk by a torpedo bomber. *Quiberon* was also one of the seven destroyers mentioned by Cunningham for its work in defending coastal shipping in its passage through submarine-infested waters to Bone, Force 'Q's advanced base.

'Torch' paved the way for the opening of the Mediterranean to through shipping once more. Its restoration as an Imperial line of communication made it only appropriate that Australia should contribute to the escort forces. Two Australian Minesweeping Flotillas were formed at Alexandria in May 1943, each composed of four *Bathurst* class AMS. The 21st Flotilla was formed of HMA Ships *Gawler, Ipswich, Lismore* and *Maryborough* and the 22nd of HMA Ships *Geraldton, Cessnock, Cairns* and *Wollongong*. The ships were attached to various escort groups for convoy work, first individually later as flotillas. Both flotillas supported the invasion of Sicily. The air threat was serious both in these operations and in the escort of through convoys but the *Bathurst* class now had sufficient AA armament to cope. After the surrender of Italy all but *Gawler, Maryborough* and *Ipswich* departed for the Indian Ocean. The last named was involved in the Dodecanese fiasco but escaped damage and passed south through Suez with *Gawler* at the end of October. It was left to *Maryborough* to be the last RAN warship in the Mediterranean; she arrived at Suez on 21 November 1943.

The use of the Mediterranean for shipping was a belated vindication of the effort the forces of the British Commonwealth put into the theatre between 1940–43. Naturally Australian assets played a significant and distinguished role in this campaign but serious questions must be posed, especially from the Australian perspective, about how well-advised strategically the Mediterranean really was. It absorbed and diverted strength that was desperately needed to contain Japan and for what purpose? To knock out the weakest Axis partner and get an Allied army eventually to the foothills of the Alps. Defending Middle East oil did not require either a major North African campaign (major that is for the British) nor the expensive sustenance of Malta that was usually more damaging to the RN and RAF than it was to Hitler and Mussolini.[28] Essentially the Mediterranean was a diversion from the only strategy that would have stood a chance of sustaining the British Empire, a due concentration on Japan and the Far East as planned pre-war. Eventual victory in the Mediterranean was thus bought at a very high price; the loss of the British Empire, about whose survival the war as a whole was supposed to have been fought.

7
Savo in retrospect

Bruce Loxton

In the last days of June 1942 the American Chiefs of Staff decided to begin the counterattack against the Japanese on 1 August by capturing, in the southern Solomons, the port of Tulagi and the site for an airfield on Guadalcanal as a first step towards Rabaul. Preparations had barely got underway when it was found that the Japanese were making rapid progress with the building of a major air base on the same site. There was therefore no time to spare. However pleas for delay from the commander of the South-West Pacific, General MacArthur, and of the South Pacific, Vice-Admiral Ghormley, both of whom believed that we could not succeed, resulted in D-Day being delayed until 7 August. A further delay was requested but refused.

An expeditionary force of some 75 ships, including three aircraft carriers carrying 256 aircraft, one battleship, thirteen cruisers and the First US Marine Division was assembled in the Fiji Islands in late July 1942. The Australian cruisers HMA Ships *Australia*, *Canberra* and *Hobart* were present, forming part of the transports' screen of cruisers and destroyers commanded by Rear-Admiral Crutchley VC, DSC. The RAAF was represented by five Hudson aircraft temporarily based on a fighter strip on Milne Bay. Their task was to search the approaches to the Solomons from Rabaul. The Solomon Islands south of Bougainville were covered by American shore- and water-based aircraft and by carrier aircraft.

Based on Rabaul were a large number of fighters and bombers, all capable of reaching Guadalcanal. Also available to the Japanese area commander, Vice-Admiral Mikawa, was a force of five heavy cruisers and some light cruisers and destroyers; a force much smaller than that of the Allies but balanced to a degree by an ability to fight at night which far transcended that of the Allies. The Allies were totally unaware of this expertise.

When the Expeditionary Force assembled in Fiji on 26 July a meeting of the senior American officers present was called by the expedition's commander,

HMAS Canberra *leaving Wellington for Guadalcanal, 22 July 1942. The heavy cruiser was built for Australia and commissioned on 9 July 1924.* Canberra *and her sister ship* Australia *were armed with eight 8-inch and four 4-inch guns, four 2-pounder pom-poms and eight 21-inch torpedo tubes.* Australia *survived the war and remained in commission until 1954. (US National Archives 80-G–13454A)*

Vice-Admiral Fletcher. Those present were surprised to hear that he had no confidence in a successful outcome and that he was not willing to risk his carriers in the assault area for more than two days. After an acrimonious debate, he reluctantly agreed to stay for three days though General Vandergrift, the Marines' commander, told him they would need carrier support for five or more. In the event he withdrew the carriers after two days for reasons that do him no credit.

Bad weather allowed the expedition to arrive undetected off the beaches on 7 August, just five weeks after the Chiefs of Staff decision. The Marines quickly achieved their objectives against strong opposition on Tulagi but virtually none on Guadalcanal where they found an almost completed air base within five days of commissioning.

Over the next two days Japanese responses were quick and positive. Three air raids were carried out on the transports, submarines were dispatched to the area and a striking force, lead by Mikawa, of five heavy cruisers, two light cruisers and a destroyer was assembled. There was considerable misgiving in Tokyo about the proposed strike but, in the end, the decision was left to Mikawa who had no doubt that all the years of training in night fighting would pay off. He was more worried about the navigational hazards in the area, for the region was poorly charted.

By dark on 7 August, Mikawa was on his way. Passing round Buka Island, he waited for a while off the east coast of Bougainville before heading at high speed for Guadalcanal. Arriving there soon after midnight on the night of 8 August, the Japanese fell upon the unsuspecting Allies who, as a result, lost four fine heavy cruisers—*Canberra, Vincennes, Quincy* and *Astoria*—and over a thousand American, Australian and British lives. Japanese casualties were in the order of 100.

The Japanese had had to steam, in daylight, through hundreds of miles of waters under the surveillance of Allied aircraft and submarines. They had been seen on several occasions. And yet they were able to achieve complete surprise. Why? And why had the Expeditionary Force suffered what has been described as a galling defeat, a debacle, a shameful defeat, a bloody shambles and an object lesson in how not to fight?

As time passed, rumours flourished and generally speaking the Navy thought that *Canberra* should have done better. As my own career progressed I came across a number of reports and books on the battle but nothing I read fully satisfied me. What I did not realise for some considerable time was that official accounts of the battle were flawed as they contained not only errors in interpretation of facts but also serious factual errors. In spite of appearances, the battle and the circumstances that brought it about had not been fully and objectively investigated. This was true not only of the part played by *Canberra* but also of that played by MacArthur's Allied Air Forces Command which included the RAAF Hudsons.

In 1959 I spent a year at the USN War College at Newport, Rhode Island, where I was subjected to a study of the Battle of Savo based entirely on an analysis of that battle by the Naval War College. My tutor was Commodore Bates, who had led the team that produced it. He regarded our Admiral Crutchley, the RAAF search aircraft, RAAF communications and *Canberra* as being in large part responsible for our defeat; views that were shared on the whole by the naval historian, Samuel Morison, who produced his book *The Struggle for Guadalcanal* at much the same time.

Bates claimed that an RAAF aircrew, after wrongly identifying some of the Japanese ships, had not reported what they had seen until after they had completed their mission, landed and had their tea. RAAF communications had been such that the report was not received by the ships off Guadalcanal until dusk. Crutchley's positioning of his ships to protect the transports had been seriously at fault. *Canberra*, the first ship to be engaged by the enemy, had made no attempt to warn other ships of their presence and had not been able to return their fire because the guns were not loaded.

The analysis on which the study was based was classified 'Confidential' and was not itself made available. Indeed it was not declassified by the War College and released to Australia until 1971. My arguments against some of those hypotheses were therefore largely based on an innate belief that we Australians and our RN Admiral could not have done as badly as we were led to believe. At the time I thought that I had not made much of an impression, but the following year Savo was not studied.

Had I known then that five years previously Bates had prevented the release of that analysis to the Australian Government for reasons that he would only give *personally* to his Director of Naval Intelligence, I might well have been more searching in my questioning, but I didn't, and I wasn't. In fact I knew nothing of his denial of information to Australians until as recently as December 1993. Be that as it may, my experience at the War College caused me to be more critical in my research; research that ultimately led me to write *The Shame of Savo*, for I found an extraordinary and widespread concatenation of errors and shortcomings, both human and systemic.

The War College, Morison and others had made considerable use of a report by Admiral Hepburn dated May 1943. Hepburn, who had been CNO pre-war, had been instructed by Admiral King, the wartime head of the American Navy, to investigate, informally, the circumstances surrounding the loss of the four heavy cruisers. King had done this because he was concerned at the lack of information available to him on the battle. His thirst for information became so intense that when the opportunity occurred he would send for quite junior officers who had taken part and interrogate them. Eventually, having received no comprehensive report of the battle from his Admirals by the end of December, he decided to find out for himself; hence Hepburn's mission.

In the context of 1943, Hepburn's report was admirable but as a document on which to base post-war accounts of the battle it had several major weaknesses: it lacked any input from Japanese records; it lacked any input from RAAF elements; and its scope was restricted to matters relating to the loss of the cruisers. It barely touched on problems within the Allies' command, communications and the conduct of the destroyers that took part in the battle. Finally, and crucially from the Australian point of view, it contained no information from Australian sources that were dated after August 1942. Hepburn was therefore unaware of the argument that developed in Australia regarding the causes of the loss of *Canberra*.

Of the four War College criticisms mentioned earlier, I disagree absolutely with two—Crutchley's positioning of his ships and the part played by *Canberra*. There is, I believe, substance in the criticism of the RAAF communications system because the reports of the two aircraft that saw Mikawa that morning were delayed to the extent that they did not reach the ships off Guadalcanal until dusk. However the fault did not lie entirely with Australians— RAAF communication personnel and aircrew were unaware of the operations off Guadalcanal. Incredibly, they had not been told of the landings because of an order from the American commander of MacArthur's air forces, Lieutenant-General Brett, who was worried about security. As a result they thought that they were supporting routine operations of our forces in New Guinea and had no idea of the urgent need of the forces off Guadalcanal for intelligence. Brett's decision must be among the silliest of the war and is partly the reason why I dedicated my book to those who lost their lives in *Canberra* as a result of Allied ineptitude, because *ineptitude* includes a measure of silliness.

There was also some justification for the criticism of RAAF reconnaissance but once again there were mitigating circumstances, not the least of which was that the two aircrews concerned had only just finished their operational training. The first aircraft to see the Japanese made a crucial error in reporting the sighting of three cruisers, three destroyers and two seaplane tenders or gunboats rather then seven cruisers and one destroyer. This error was in part due to the failure of the same Lieutenant-General Brett to improve ship recognition training after the Battle of the Coral Sea in May 1942. There *Australia* had been very inaccurately bombed by American Army aircraft. The incident had been reported to Brett who refused to believe that any such incident had occurred, *in spite of incontrovertible photographic evidence*. He prohibited further discussion on the matter. As a result no action was taken to improve training in ship recognition and to provide recognition aids for reconnaissance aircraft and for airfields such as Milne Bay.

The Naval War College's analysis was, however, quite wrong in stating that the crew had continued with their mission for another four hours after sighting the Japanese; that they had made no attempt to report what they had seen; and that after landing, before making any report, they had had tea. In fact there is positive evidence that they attempted to report by radio (for their report was intercepted by the Japanese), that they returned immediately to Milne Bay and that, after landing, they immediately reported what they had seen.

Criticism of the RAAF would have been on much firmer ground had some attention been given to the handling of the report of the second aircraft that saw Mikawa that morning. The pilot's log book recorded the sighting and that the aircraft had been hit by AA fire. Apparently, when they tried to report by radio, they were silenced by their base and, after they eventually landed, the pilot's report of having seen six cruisers and two destroyers, which was very close to the truth, was altered by RAAF base staff to read just two cruisers, two destroyers and one other small ship. This report was even longer in transit than its predecessor.

Americans in general, with the notable exceptions of Admirals King and Hepburn, were critical of Crutchley's dispositions for the prevention of a Japanese entry into the Sound because he split his six heavy cruisers into two groups, one patrolling to the north-east and the other to the south-east of Savo Island. In those days, surface warning radar was in its infancy and *Canberra* was the only heavy cruiser so fitted. Her radar's performance was, however, inadequate to ensure that an enemy force could be engaged before opening fire on the transports. This could only be achieved if the heavy cruisers were operating in two groups, one patrolling each entrance into the Sound.

There was another valid reason for not concentrating the six ships. Three of them had never operated with Crutchley or indeed with any Australian ship. Furthermore, there was at that time no common Allied night-fighting doctrine. This lack would have made control of a mixed six-unit force at night more than just a little difficult. In the event, even the Japanese, with a common doctrine frequently exercised, became disorganised in the course of the battle. The Allied situation would have been exacerbated by the fact that while the American cruisers *Vincennes*, *Quincy* and *Astoria* were fitted with a voice radio for tactical control, to the detriment of their ability to communicate visually, *Australia*, *Canberra* and the American *Chicago*, which had been with Crutchley for several months, were not and relied on visual signalling. Crutchley was therefore of the opinion that the two groups of cruisers were operationally incompatible at night. This, and the need to cover both entrances properly, convinced him that the well-known principle in war of concentration should, on that occasion, be disregarded.

Crutchley was also criticised for placing only two destroyers, *Blue* and *Ralph Talbot*, on picket duty to seaward of Savo Island. In view of the perceived submarine threat, his reasons for doing this were sound, but in the context of Savo the matter is of academic interest only as the Japanese passed unseen within a mile of *Blue*. Visibility in the vicinity of Savo was patchy but *Blue* logged it as being eight miles at the time. It has been said, with some justification, that the enemy would have had to have collided with her before they were seen. Most definitely, therefore, Crutchley's allocation of only two destroyers to the picket line was not a factor in the defeat.

And finally I come to the sinking of *Canberra*. As those who have read *The Shame of Savo* will know, I have come to the conclusion that *Canberra* was torpedoed by the American destroyer *Bagley* in the opening stages of the battle. This caused a total loss of power before we could open fire. The guns *were* in fact loaded and attempts *were* made to inform other ships of the enemy's approach, both by visual signal and by radio. What I believe happened is shown in Figure 7.2.

It would be reasonable to ask why it was that the possibility that *Bagley* torpedoed *Canberra* was not mooted years ago. I would reply that I believe that it should have been. The possibility was almost certainly appreciated by Commander Ramsey (later Rear-Admiral) who was Admiral Hepburn's assistant in 1943. In a letter to the American naval historian Morison in the late 1940s and in a conversation in 1960 in Washington with Rear-Admiral Gatacre who, as a Commander, had been Crutchley's Staff Officer Operations at Savo, Ramsey as good as admitted it. There cannot be any doubt that the Naval War College analysts in 1950 should also have realised what could have happened because of a diagram, a portion of which is reproduced in Figure 7.1, that I found in their analysis. As can be seen *Canberra* was shown to be turning into *Bagley*'s torpedoes. Evidence that they probably did is strengthened by Bates' reluctance to release the document to the Australian Government. In 1943 Hepburn probably did not pursue the matter

Figure 7.1: Battle of Savo Island

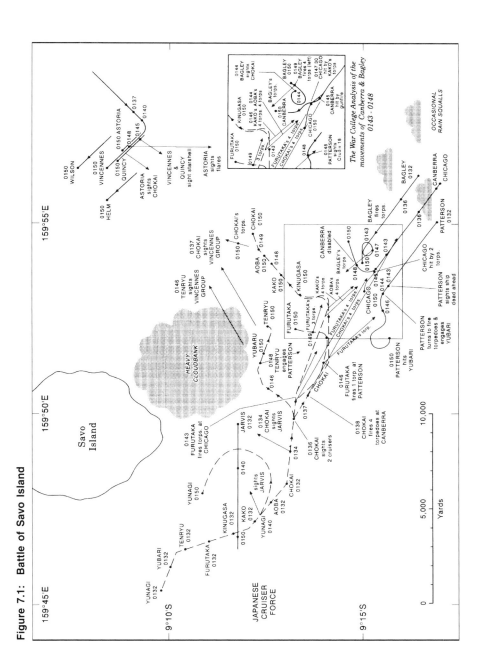

Figure 7.2: Movements of Canberra and Bagley

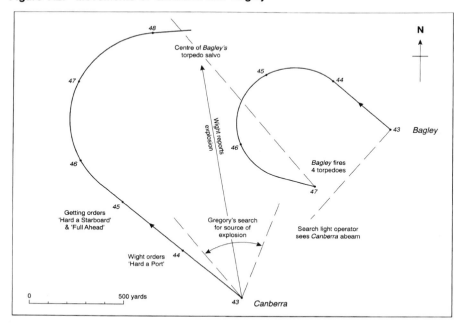

because he appreciated the damage that would have been done to morale if it were known that *Canberra* had been immobilised by an American ship. In retrospect, on those grounds, I believe that he would have been right but Ramsey, in his conversation with Gatacre, inferred that there was another and less creditable motive for not pursuing the matter. According to Ramsey, Admiral Nimitz was reluctant to accept that the defeat could have resulted from any American shortcomings, believing in fact that Crutchley was to blame. He was reluctant to accept otherwise so that it was to spare his feelings that the report of the inquiry was limited in its scope. Such hypothesis does neither Hepburn nor Nimitz credit, but it would explain why Ramsey was reluctant, even after the war when Nimitz was still alive, 'to spill the beans'. There was no justification for such a cover-up to be continued when the strategic need for it had disappeared. Figure 7.1 explains, but does not excuse, why Bates withheld the Naval War College's analysis from Australians for as long as he could.

I was among a group of badly wounded men who were told, on their return to Sydney, that we should have felt ashamed of ourselves for being sunk without firing a shot in our defence and, although I didn't much care for the remark, I had to go along with it. But now, if anyone were to reproach me in a similar fashion, I would, among other things, reply that any feeling of shame has been well and truly exorcised. Feelings of guilt should lie elsewhere than among the survivors of *Canberra*.

8
South-West Pacific Sea Frontiers: Seapower in the Australian context

David Stevens

One of the first problems confronting historians of the Australian Navy in World War II is to determine exactly what the RAN achieved. Though it seems that none has so far suggested that the members of the RAN were anything other than loyal and courageous, the service itself has been the subject of much more critical examination. Portraying the RAN as a small wartime adjunct of two great power navies with world roles, some historians have expressed doubts about the RAN's effect on the war. By balancing the total Australian warship tonnage lost, against enemy warship tonnage sunk by the RAN, they have also questioned the RAN's efficiency in carrying out its allotted tasks.[1]

It is certainly true that Australian vessels seldom operated as a purely Australian force and, unsurprisingly, in comparison with the British and American navies the RAN's participation was relatively modest. It is also unfortunately true that many of the best remembered episodes of Australia's naval war surround tragic incidents. The loss of HMAS *Sydney* to an inferior enemy, and the loss of HMAS *Canberra* without firing a shot come readily to mind. Even two of the RAN's greatest epics of courage are derived from the sinkings of HMA Ships *Perth* and *Yarra* in the face of overwhelming odds. In this light, the victory of *Sydney* over the *Bartolomeo Colleoni*, though heroic in its own right, does not seem to adequately restore the scales.

However, to attempt to assess the RAN's achievements by quoting ship losses, brief engagements, and simple statistics, is to misunderstand much of what a navy is designed to achieve. The practice of maritime power is seldom about short but glorious sea battles; more often it is about the application of slow, steady and ultimately exhausting, pressure; the strangulation of an enemy's resources while at the same time protecting your own. The RAN may have traded blows infrequently, but even when not directly engaging the enemy, the navy was on call, supporting and sustaining Allied operations.

This chapter examines one of the clearest examples of the successful Australian use of maritime power during World War II. At the same time, it is perhaps the least well remembered. The South-West Pacific Sea Frontiers Command directed the prolonged application of naval forces in a way that was both vitally important to the defence of maritime Australia and to the land campaign in New Guinea. There may not have been a single decisive battle for command, but there was a continuous struggle by both sides to keep the sea for their own use while denying it to their adversary. At the time, General Douglas MacArthur's efficient publicity machine ensured that the naval role was ignored. The tradition that has built up since has consistently overlooked the RAN's contribution in favour of Australia's land and air operations in New Guinea. This chapter is an initial attempt to reassess that tradition.

South-West Pacific Area

For the first two years, World War II was essentially a European conflict, so problems of support for the Army and protection of shipping were not crucial to the defence of Australia. However, once Japan had entered the war the environment was radically and irrevocably altered. Australia was under direct threat, and it was very soon America rather than Britain to whom Australia looked for security.

As the only viable Pacific base after the initial Japanese conquests, Australia became vital to American plans for a counteroffensive against Japan. The directive that formed the South-West Pacific Area (SWPA) in April 1942 gave MacArthur, as Supreme Commander, exclusive strategic and operational responsibility for Australia's defence. All orders and instructions issued by MacArthur to other national forces in the SWPA were to be considered as emanating from their respective governments. Even Prime Minister Curtin acknowledged that participation in what was a unique command structure meant that Australia had in effect surrendered a part of her sovereignty.

The Naval Board was now in an interesting position. Before the war, as the operating authority for the Australia Station, the ACNB had acted in many ways as a local CinC for the British Admiralty. Yet the Board had still retained direct responsibility to the Commonwealth Government for Australia's maritime defence and the protection of trade. Moreover after 1939, though RAN units were routinely serving immediately under the Admiralty, the Board had continued to exercise control over the administration and disposition of its vessels in Pacific and Far Eastern waters. Even after the establishment of the ABDA Area in January 1942, when command of RAN units operating in the Malayan/Netherlands East Indies theatre passed to the relevant ABDA commander, the ACNB had maintained operational control of units in Australian waters.[2] But a month later the situation had fundamentally changed. In February, Vice-Admiral H.F. Leary USN assumed command of Allied Naval Forces in the Australian–New

Figure 8.1: Australian Naval Command Organisation, April 1942–September 1945

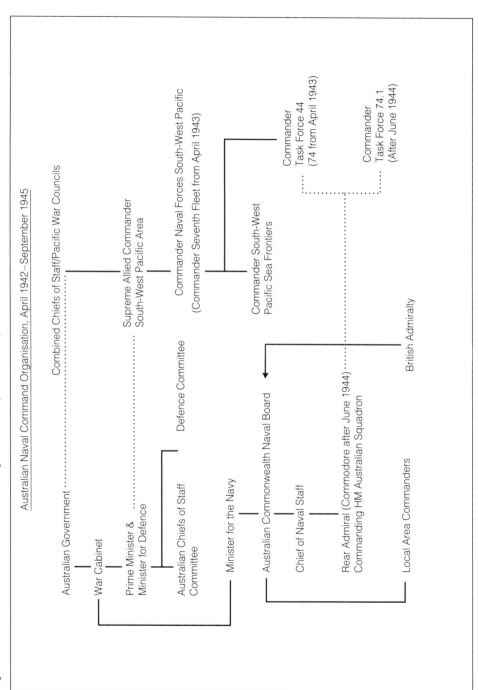

Australian Naval Command Organisation, April 1942 – September 1945

The Japanese submarine I–29 was one of five that took part in the midget submarine attack on Sydney on the night of 31 May–1 June 1942. I–29's aircraft carried out a flight over Sydney on 23 May and confirmed the presence of warships in the harbour. A week earlier the I–29 had carried out the first submarine attack off the Australian east coast when she shelled the Soviet steamer Wellen. *(D. Stevens)*

Zealand Area as Commander ANZAC Force. In April, on MacArthur's appointment as Supreme Commander, Leary became one of his three environmental commanders as Commander South-West Pacific Force, also known as Commander Allied Naval Forces South-West Pacific Area (CANFSWPA).

Leary thus became responsible to MacArthur for all naval operations in the SWPA, including the operational control of RAN units in the area and the maintenance of sea communications.[3] Having relinquished this control the ACNB could have been easily left as a purely administrative authority, the Board thereafter solely looking after naval facilities and supporting operations afloat. However, such a role would have suited neither the aspirations of the Naval Board nor the maintenance of a workable security relationship between America and Australia. Thus, by delegation from Leary, the ACNB retained responsibility for the protection of coastal shipping and the conduct of convoys off Australia.

The ACNB, under the guidance of Admiral Sir Guy Royle, Chief of Naval Staff, discharged its defence-of-trade task using a series of Port Directors, District Naval Officers and Naval Officers-in-Charge (NOIC) of areas. It was the NOICs who dealt directly with the escorts allocated to the convoy system, and dispersed them to the various ports as directed by the ACNB. Nevertheless, as a subordinate command, the Naval Board would always first seek concurrence for its planned dispositions from CANFSWPA.

The threat to shipping in Australian waters took some months to develop. A routine coastal convoy system did not begin on the east coast until June 1942, a month after the first escorted convoy from the mainland to New Guinea, and a week after the Sydney Harbour raid by Japanese midget submarines. In May

The anti-submarine ratings of HMAS Arunta *pose on the upper deck of their Australian-built destroyer. In the background can be seen the badly damaged transport* SS Malaita, *at anchor after being torpedoed by the Japanese submarine RO 33 on 29 August 1942 outside Port Moresby.* Arunta *was escorting* Malaita *at the time and in a series of four depth charge attacks destroyed the attacker. (V. Lewis)*

there had been only one escort allocated to the convoy system and, though this had risen to sixteen by June, a lack of suitable vessels was to be a continuous problem.[4] With so few available, there was a reluctance to arrange designated escort groups and vessels were initially allocated in an *ad hoc* manner with each ship regarded as an independent command.[5]

The Naval Board maintained responsibility for the defence of shipping in most Australian areas; however, the increasing build-up of land forces in New Guinea made the protection and routing of vessels in the vital North-Eastern Area a particular priority. On 11 September 1942 Vice-Admiral A.S. Carpender USN succeeded Vice-Admiral Leary as CANFSWPA. In one of his first acts on taking up command, Carpender informed Royle that he would be assuming control of all convoys proceeding to New Guinea.[6] Though the southern limit of the North-Eastern Area was somewhat in doubt, it was intended that CAN-FSWPA's control should broadly cover shipping in support of military operations, and generally assumed that direction extended north from Brisbane. Nevertheless, Carpender could only exercise control through the NOICs, so close Australian naval involvement was still guaranteed.

Northward-bound convoys were sailed by NOIC Brisbane or Townsville (also known as NOIC North-Eastern Area) in accordance with military priority.

91

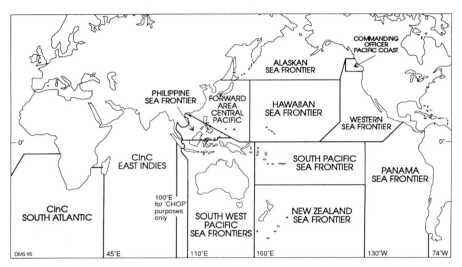

Map 8.1: *Boundaries of Allied naval areas for purposes of reporting merchant vessels and convoys in 1945*

Sailings were arranged so that the troops and cargo carried in the ships arrived at ports of discharge as required by the Army commander using a 'call forward procedure'.[7] At the same time it was the NOIC's responsibility to avoid harbour concentrations of shipping to minimise the danger from air attack. All shipping loaded with defence cargo sailed in escorted convoy from the Grafton Passage, with not more than three ships escorted by one escort vessel if practicable.

Soon there was a complete system of convoys stretching from Melbourne to advanced New Guinea bases and Darwin, with special escort cover always arranged by Royle for troop movements.[8] The coastal convoy system remained in force until 1944 and proved extremely successful. During 1942 there were 211 separate convoys, made up of 1505 ships, run between Australian ports, and another 167 ships in 41 convoys between the mainland and New Guinea.[9] Only one vessel, the Panamanian SS *Guatemala*, was sunk in these convoys, and she was straggling.[10] During 1943 the increasing requirements of the Allied build-up resulted in a total of 748 convoys and 4155 ships being run, with a monthly average of another 60 ships requiring independent escort to forward areas.[11] In addition—since not all shipping movements remained within the area—important overseas ships, including American Army and Naval transports, were given escort to the limits of the SWPA.

Sea Frontiers Command

The routing and reporting of Allied merchant vessels was a worldwide concern. The various control authorities could offer shipping protection through a combination of combatant forces, convoy escorts, air and intelligence units. Furthermore, to actually avoid enemy attacks the control authorities could also diversify routing, open new routes or divert ships on their assigned routes. In the Atlantic the Americans had found the development of evasive routing techniques particularly effective, and in early 1943 the USN decided to introduce similar methods of merchant ship protection into the whole Pacific area. The Pacific was therefore divided into control areas called 'Sea Frontiers', corresponding where practicable to the strategic subdivisions.[12]

The Australian Sea Frontiers Command was initially established by Admiral Carpender on 4 March 1943.[13] Two weeks later it was renamed as the South-West Pacific Sea Frontiers (SWPSF) and formally established on 25 March.[14] Under the terms of the British–United States Routing Agreement, it had been directed that routing in the SWPA should be done using the agencies available to the ACNB and operating under its direction. Responsibility as Commander South-West Pacific Sea Frontiers (CSWPSF) was thus assigned to the First Naval Member, Admiral Royle.

Royle's instructions charged him with: the safe conduct and routing of all coastal shipping; shipping to and from contiguous areas; and routine shipping in support of military operations.[15] Under the Sea Frontiers system Carpender elected only to direct protection of shipping in connection with special military operations. Thus Royle could now exercise operational control of all escort and minesweeping vessels otherwise assigned to him. Where necessary, the vessels available to Royle's command were supplemented for a specific task or period from an appropriate Task Force. Normally Carpender would need to authorise the request, but on occasion Royle or his representative was given approval to make requests directly to the Task Group Commanders. In practice operational control continued to be exercised through the various NOICs, and, in the case of convoys and escorts proceeding from one area to another, would change at a prearranged time based on the expected time of passing the dividing line between areas. Instructions for diversion of merchant vessels proceeding independently would also usually be issued by Royle. But although Royle might order a convoy to be sailed on a definite route, it was the responsibility of the NOIC of the area concerned to order any convoy diversions, either before or during the passage.[16]

Off New Guinea and northern Australia the prime threat against shipping was air attack. However, off the remainder of the coast it continued to come from submarines. The SWPSF had been formed just as Japanese submarine attacks were reaching a peak. Having belatedly decided to increase pressure on Allied communications the Japanese sent four boats from the 3rd Submarine Squadron to operate off the east coast between April and May 1943. In a three-week period the Japanese sank seven merchant ships and damaged another two. Four of these vessels were in convoy. The offensive was not unexpected by Royle, as radio intelligence had provided prior warning of broad Japanese intentions. Nevertheless, the sinkings caused consternation within the Australian Shipping Control

The AMS, HMAS Gympie. *On 17 March 1943* Gympie *was acting as escort for convoy BT.44 when the convoy was attacked by the Japanese submarine* I–6 *off Sandy Cape.* Gympie *with an RAAF Anson drove off the attacker without loss to the convoy. On 1 April* Gympie *in her role as a minesweeper successfully swept a field of acoustic mines laid by* I–6 *in the approaches to Brisbane. (RAN)*

Board and Department of Commerce. Shipping was in short supply worldwide and even minor losses had the potential to disrupt economic and military plans. The situation with regard to Australian iron ore and coal shipments was regarded as particularly serious.[17]

On 28 April eight scheduled convoys were cancelled because of the high level of enemy submarine activity; while on 13 May, Royle announced that the number of coastal convoys would in future be halved to allow escort vessels to be doubled.[18] According to Royle the main naval activity in the SWPA was now the provision of escort for convoys and independent shipping to New Guinea.[19] In June 56 warships were allocated to the escort system.[20] That same month the RAAF recorded 537 sorties flown in support of 84 convoys and 45 independently routed ships, and a further 165 sorties flown on searches and reconnaissance flights.[21]

Though in mid-1943 the tide of battle in the Atlantic was about to turn against the submarine, there was no such confidence in the SWPA. Despite an increasing array of forces it seemed to many that the SWPA anti-submarine effort was in crisis. Carpender's Commander Escort and Minecraft Vessels (CTF 78) noted that Fleet anti-submarine forces, including the RAN, were far behind in the methods and objectives of anti-submarine warfare.[22] In the Advisory War Council, W. M. Hughes, leader of the United Australia Party, submitted a damning statement regarding the efficiency of both naval and air anti-submarine operations on the east coast of Australia.[23] Commander H. Newcombe, Commanding Officer of HMAS *Rushcutter*, the Australian anti-submarine training establishment, wrote to the Naval Board highlighting the lack of success in countering enemy submarine action.[24] Carpender and Royle both looked more closely at the SWPA and found many organisational problems.

Despite the formation of SWPSF there was no single authority designated for the control of escorts. Effort was being duplicated, with vessels being assigned both to the Sea Frontiers Command and to other Task Forces. The escorts themselves were mostly of an unsatisfactory type. They tended to be slow, incapable of operating asdic in the conditions prevailing off the coast, lacked efficient communications and few were fitted with radar.[25] Training was conducted largely upon independent national lines. USN ships in the area had no training submarine or training ship; while the Australians had only one submarine, *K9*, and she was in such poor condition that she only ever spent 31 days at sea during her time in the RAN.[26] The Australian training ship HMAS *Kybra* was not fitted with USN equipment and had spent much of her time either on operational duties or in refit.[27]

Difficulty was also being experienced in the exchange of shipping information between Royle and Carpender and the contiguous areas. Communications westward used British codes, and eastward US codes. Often the same message had to be enciphered in a variety of different formats. At one stage the level of classification of US shipping and ship movement reports from the American West Coast and Panama prevented them being seen by the Australians. To improve the situation it was eventually found necessary to set up a special USN coding unit at the Naval Board Headquarters at Victoria Barracks in Melbourne.[28]

Cooperation between the RAN and RAAF also left much to be desired. Because enemy submarine operations had been sporadic there had been no definite effort made to assign air units to a coastal command similar to the United Kingdom's 'Western Approaches'. Instead, in one principal port in each Australian area there was an Air Operations Room from which air and surface operations could in theory be coordinated. However, air operations were dependent on the limited equipment and armament available to aircraft in the area. Off the east coast this often meant the employment of light bombers and training aircraft rather than specialised reconnaissance or anti-submarine types. There were also differences of opinion with regard to tactics, the RAAF officially preferring 'offensive' sweeps and searches of threatened areas, rather than the supposedly 'defensive policy' of convoy escort.[29] Further hampering cooperation, there was usually no direct communication available between air and surface units and signals had to pass through a shore station.[30]

As a final complication the Australian services' intelligence organisations were remote from each other, with surface direction finding (D/F) intelligence concentrated in Melbourne and the air D/F centre at Brisbane. Though the organisations attempted to work together, the separation complicated the problem of close coordinated intelligence. In May 1943 the RAAF complained that the

RAN fixing organisation was being staffed only during the day, thus causing unacceptable delays.[31] Another complaint in July noted that a nine-hour delay had caused a search area to increase from 7800 to 38 500 square miles.[32]

In a bid to find a solution to some of these problems Carpender proposed the establishment of an Anti-Submarine Warfare Unit for the SWPA under Royle's direction. The unit would be set up within Navy Office and staffed by RAN, USN and RAAF anti-submarine specialists. It was planned that the unit produce an agreed attack and signal procedure, an anti-submarine training program for escort vessels and Task Forces, and control the dissemination of anti-submarine information from all sources.[33] The Naval Board was supportive, but maintained that training should continue to be conducted on independent national lines.[34] The Board appeared to believe that the Australian Navy had a better capability for training than the USN and argued that suitable publications could adequately produce a common doctrine for coordinated operations.

The Australian opinion prevailed and though personnel from USN ships visited *Rushcutter* for team-training, coordinated RAN–USN training at sea does not appear to have been conducted on a regular basis.[35] Nevertheless, by July a draft of combined procedures had been produced; while by September plans were advanced to ensure that before commencing convoy duties all newly commissioned RAN escort vessels were allowed at least three weeks uninterrupted work-up under the direction of Commander (D) Sydney. In contrast, USN escort vessels were to be given at least ten days intensive training under CTF 78 on first arrival in the area.[36]

In comparison with other areas under submarine threat, the most significant development still missing from the SWPSF was the establishment of escort groups. By September 1943 Royle had 41 RAN and 17 USN vessels allocated to escort duties around Australia and New Guinea. Thinly spread between the various areas it was felt that designated groups were still not feasible, but that without groups, maximum value was not being obtained from escorts and that the development of teamwork was impracticable. Not until more anti-submarine vessels became available was it envisioned that greater protection would be possible, particularly in focal areas, and that separate striking forces could then be stationed at selected ports.[37]

The target for March 1944 was for an additional 14 RAN vessels and 30 USN Destroyer Escorts (DE). With these forces it was hoped to have six escort groups operating from Sydney, five from Milne Bay, three each from Brisbane and Townsville, and two from Darwin. Single escorts would be allocated to Melbourne and Fremantle. Composition of each group would vary according to assets in the area, but averaged one frigate and four corvettes. In the major ports of Sydney, Brisbane and Townsville it was planned to base a special 'Fast Group' comprising up to six DEs and six frigates.[38]

By this stage of the war MacArthur was firmly on the offensive and, by conducting a series of amphibious assaults, Allied troops proceeded to outmanoeuvre or bypass Japanese strong points and move inexorably northward. These assaults were made possible by the formation of Rear-Admiral Daniel Barbey's 7th Amphibious Force (TF 76) and it was shipping in support of this force that received highest priority for protection. The provision of escort for Barbey's forces highlighted the problem of duplicated effort, and in January 1944 a joint RAN–USN conference reiterated that to avoid confusion all escort vessels should be combined into a single command under CSWPSF. Escort groups could then be assigned to TF 76 for limited periods for duties in connection with the execution of amphibious landings. On completion of the landings, ships would revert to the escort command.

No doubt encouraged by reports of the success of 'Hunter–Killer' tactics in the Atlantic, the RAN–USN conference also recommended that six Catalina and six Liberator aircraft should be given up for naval operational control; thus permitting the formation of 'Hunter–Killer Groups' in the SWPA. These groups were to be organised, trained and operated as a single tactical unit. Royle's staff suggested that he should be made responsible for the operation of the Hunter–Killer Groups. Their argument was that the task of 'purely defensive escort' of shipping and the 'more offensive' killer organisation were so closely allied that it would be well to have a coordinated effort under the same commander.[39]

However, with the favourable war situation the large-scale formation of escort groups and the integration of surface and air units under the one Australian commander was not to occur. Finding themselves more and more on the defensive, the Japanese had ceased submarine operations against Australia in July 1943.[40] By November recommendations had been made that coastal convoys should be abolished south of Newcastle. Though industrial action by the Seamen's Union delayed implementation of this recommendation, it was clear that the threat in Australian waters was declining.[41] The organisation of the Sydney-based escort groups, one of the few to have been formed, was soon abandoned. In February 1944, the continued absence of enemy submarines in Australian waters led to the suspension of convoys south of Townsville. The abolition of Townsville–New Guinea Convoys followed in March, though the convoy system continued to be observed in northern New Guinea waters until late 1944.

With Australia now seen as a strategic backwater, the majority of naval forces were moved north, closer to the scene of operations. Nevertheless, both surface and air patrols were maintained at selected points, and striking forces were held in readiness. This was a wise precaution, for in September intelligence reports indicated the possibility of German submarines operating in the Fremantle area. The intelligence had been derived from a decrypted message from the German Naval CinC, Admiral Karl Dönitz, authorising a mission by two U-boats based in the Far East into Australian waters.[42] On 19 September, only five days after Dönitz released his signal, Royle directed NOIC Darwin and NOIC Sydney to transfer a total of four corvettes to the temporary operational control of NOIC Fremantle, Commodore C. Pope RAN.[43] The same day another message was sent to all NOICs ordering westbound shipping to Indian Ocean ports to be routed well dispersed so as to pass not less than 250 miles south of the coast between Albany and Cape Leeuwin.[44] Pope meanwhile promulgated plans to form a joint RAN–USN Hunter–Killer Group under his direct operational orders.[45]

The Germans eventually sent four U-boats to operate in Australian waters. Betrayed by radio intelligence, three were sunk soon after their departure from Japanese-held ports by forces directed by CANFSWPA.[46] The sole surviving U-boat, *U 862*, arrived off Cape Leeuwin on 28 November 1944. The U-boat then continued east trying to intercept shipping in the Great Australian Bight. NOIC Fremantle was not given an opportunity to deploy his Hunter–Killer Group, but Royle's diversion of merchant shipping had been successful. After her own fruitless hunt the U-boat eventually worked its way around to the east coast. Off Sydney, six weeks after her departure, the U-boat finally found and sank a merchant ship. In response Royle initiated the most intensive anti-submarine search ever seen in Australian waters. The hunt failed to find the U-boat but the activity had ensured that the U-boat's commander did not remain in the area and instead he crept away to try the quieter waters of New Zealand.

This was to be the last enemy activity off Australia, but elsewhere in the SWPA, CSWPSF's area of responsibility continued to expand. In April 1944 responsibility for the protection and routing of shipping to and from the Admiralty Islands had passed to the Sea Frontier Commander and in May it became a new sub-area. In June the North Solomons Area was established as another sub-area of SWPSF. By 2 September 1945, when the SWPA Command was abolished, the ACNB had accepted responsibility for all SWPA ocean areas from Borneo to the east, including Nauru and Ocean Islands.[47] On this date control of all RAN combat forces reverted back to the Naval Board.

Conclusions

The SWPSF was a subordinate command within the hierarchical structure of the SWPA. The Australian Navy was too small for MacArthur to have ever entertained the idea of a joint command arrangement or indeed of offering Royle the position of CANFSWPA. On a global basis the SWPA was not the highest priority for equipment allocation and for the majority of the time it was a matter of making do with the limited assets available. The SWPSF was even lower in the pecking order. Though there were problems in communications and organisation, which should have been addressed earlier than they were, the Command nevertheless carried out its responsibilities with a unity of purpose and depth of commitment that proved extremely successful. From mid-1942 maritime forces allowed the build-up of Allied strength in New Guinea that first checked then gradually pushed back the Japanese advance. From mid-1943 maritime forces were central to MacArthur's planning, playing an 'enabling' role in allowing his campaigns to take place. Without the secure and interlocking system of convoys and the efficient control of shipping there could have been no offensives in New Guinea and beyond.

Royle was not averse to making critical comments where MacArthur was concerned. In 1943 he wrote a personal letter to Carpender, in which he expressed his 'considerable concern' regarding MacArthur's policy regarding release of information to the public:

> No mention has been made of the importance that control of the sea has had, and is having, in the New Guinea campaign or in the Southwest Pacific Area generally, and the work of our ships and men is passing completely unnoticed. The result is that the men lose that encouragement by recognition which is their due. Furthermore, through lack of its attention being directed to any practical example, the public mind is becoming less and less conscious of the important role of Sea Power, and is acquiring an entirely erroneous standard of values. This is to my mind, harmful to the Navy at present and fraught with danger for the future.[48]

Despite the passage of more than fifty years we would do well to reflect on Royle's words.

9

The forgotten bases: The Royal Navies in the Pacific, 1945

David Brown

In 1995 the fiftieth anniversary of the return of peace was first commemorated in Europe. For the majority, at the time, the war ended on 8 May 1945—Victory in Europe Day—but the war in the Far East went on for another 99 days and besides the 'Forgotten Army', there were two 'Forgotten Fleets', both of which were at sea on 15 August—Victory over Japan Day.[1]

When the war ended in Europe the RN had in service 120 major warships, 846 destroyers, frigates, sloops and corvettes, 131 submarines and 729 mine-sweepers, besides over 1000 landing craft and minor war vessels including ships taken up from trade, and fishing vessels. Exclusive of the 40 RN Air Stations worldwide, which supported 69 front-line squadrons and over 200 aircraft, there were over 150 self-accounting shore bases. Nearly 800 000 men and women were in naval and Royal Marines uniforms. Such a vast force had been needed to fight on several 'fronts'—off the European and Norwegian coasts, in mid-Atlantic and the Arctic, in both basins of the Mediterranean and in the Indian Ocean; as recently as March 1945, the Pacific had also become a major active theatre for the RN.

After the occupation and liberation tasks in the first days of peace in Europe, the only active operations were those of the minesweeping flotillas and the escort groups finishing their last convoy passages or bringing in surrendering U-boats, relatively relaxed occupations compared with that of the minesweepers, faced with the task of clearing both sides' mines—prey that didn't know the meaning of 'friendly' or 'surrender'. The main Fleets west of Suez had already been stripped to the stage where, other than ships working-up for service in the Far East, there were only ten cruisers and about two dozen Fleet destroyers in home waters and the Mediterranean. Modern units earmarked for service in the Far East were being given priority for refit and rearming, but the pace of preparation was measured, rather than urgent, for it was expected in May 1945 that the war would continue well into 1946 and the Chiefs of Staff were even ready for it to be prolonged into 1947: Rapid reinforcement of the British Pacific Fleet (BPF), above that planned before VE-Day, was of less concern than the ability to sustain operations. In the event, of 70 destroyers and frigates allocated from home commands after VE-Day to the East Indies and British Pacific Fleets, none saw action before VJ-Day.

Far East plans: European run-down

The provisional timetable for operations in the East Indies foresaw the invasion of northern Malaya at the end of August 1945, followed by a leapfrogging amphibious advance down the peninsula towards Singapore, which would be captured in January 1946. This was a British theatre in which the RN, assisted by French and Dutch warships, took the maritime lead. In the Pacific, where the RN was playing the unaccustomed role of junior partner in operations, the Americans planned to mount an amphibious assault on the southern island of Kyushu in November and hoped to follow this with the decisive invasion of Honshu, in the Tokyo area, in the spring of 1946. The British Government intended that the carrier task groups of the BPF would take part in all future operations against the Japanese home islands and also wished to contribute land forces to the Honshu assault.

A number of factors combined to delay the arrival of the reinforcements. Among the most significant was the high priority given to reducing the personnel strength of the Navy, following plans made in September 1944 to demobilise the older and longer serving officers and ratings and, under the Category 'B' Scheme, to implement the government decision to transfer as many men as possible to the building trade and to certain specialist industries involved in post-war reconstruction. The first category to go included those over 50-years of age, 9600 men being discharged between 18 June and 16 July; these were followed by the more senior 'Age and Service' (Category 'A') Groups, from which 38 400 men were returned to 'civvy street' by 10 September. WRNS officers and ratings were being discharged under similar conditions, although priority was given to married ratings and to those who had volunteered for nursing training or for transfer as wardresses to the Prison Service. Under Category 'B', more than 2000 ratings were allocated to industry and 500 officers and men returned to teaching and the police forces.

These numbers could only be found by rapidly paying off ships and bases. The end of the U-boat war led to the rapid contraction of Western Approaches Command and by the end of May 159 anti-submarine escorts (17 escort destroyers, 66 sloops and frigates and 76 corvettes) had either been paid off or were alongside awaiting reduction to reserve. So great was the haste that many of those placed in Category 'C' Reserve—those that would not be needed again in this war—were stripped of no more than their secret, inflammable and valuable stores before being laid up.

Ships remaining in commission in European waters had their complements weeded to, and sometimes below, peace levels. The first review of Home Fleet complements found 1115 seamen, stokers and Royal Marines could be spared by reducing the weapons and radar crews of six cruisers and thirteen destroyers. A second review found more engine-room personnel, combed out more seamen and Royal Marines, and made inroads on the paymasters' empires. In all, nearly 2000 men were freed from the Home Fleet for discharge, transfer or re-employment.

The Admiralty had warned from the first that the pattern of discharge would not be even, that there would be shortage categories and the exigencies of the Service would result in delays. Communications and engine-room ratings were particularly unfortunate in this respect, as were medical personnel, while aircrew officers, required in increasing numbers for the eastern theatres, were in a class of their own, with the BPF alone demanding 150 replacement aircrew per month, over and above those needed to form additional squadrons for reserve air groups. The BPF nevertheless managed to return about 300 Category 'A' officers and men by mid-June, their places being taken by some of the 10 000 personnel who arrived in the theatre during April, May and June, most as crews of ships but enough to establish a barracks and drafting pool at Sydney. The East Indies Fleet showed a similar increase, but at least half of the newly arrived officers and men were in ships and squadrons working-up en route for the Pacific.

By the end of June, 150 700 officers and men and 2200 WRNS—a fifth of the strength of the Navy—were serving in the Indian Ocean and Pacific and more than two-thirds of them were serving afloat. The ratio in the BPF was even higher, with four men at sea for every one ashore. This high proportion of personnel in ships (in home waters the number had been about even) was due in part to the relatively large number of big warships in the BPF—three battleships, eight cruisers, five armoured fleet carriers, three light fleet carriers and seven escort carriers—but it owed more to the nature of the main base and to the 'afloat support' philosophy of operations that the Fleet had been obliged to adopt.

Not included in these manpower figures are the Dominion navies' contribution—cruisers from New Zealand and Canada and destroyers and minesweeping corvettes from Australia. 'British' Pacific Fleet is a misnomer—rather, it was an 'Imperial Pacific Fleet'.

The Australian base

As early as 27 December 1941 the Admiralty had communicated to the ACNB a scheme for developing two Fleet Bases and two Operational Bases in Australian waters. The Operational Bases, at Darwin and Hobart, were to be able to support a squadron consisting of a battleship, a fleet carrier, three cruisers and a flotilla of destroyers, while the Fleet Bases at Sydney and Fremantle should each be

The East Indies Fleet

The East Indies Fleet was more fortunate in working from a more developed base and over shorter distances, and it was not called upon to perform sustained high-intensity operations on the scale experienced in the Pacific; indeed, between VE- and VJ-Days, it made only four major sorties to deliver strikes. In the course of these it sank a heavy cruiser and destroyed a large proportion of the Japanese Army's remaining aircraft in southern Thailand and Malaya.

It might have been expected that nearly 200 years of occupancy and three years of war would have turned Trincomalee into a fully developed base, or would at least have provided the necessary facilities for the Fleet in the Indian Ocean. In practice, this was not the case, particularly with regard to recreational and leisure facilities but also in the provision, in a huge anchorage, of such essential resources as sufficient boats for traffic between ships and the shore. (There were also some prejudices to be overcome—the aircraft maintenance ship *Unicorn* was in 1944 banished to join the submariners in an outermost corner because a senior officer objected to the noise of her aero-engine test runs.) A floating dock capable of taking the largest ship in the Fleet had been delivered in 1944 but failed to live up to its promise at the first attempt—thereafter, the largest ships that could be docked in Ceylon were light cruisers. Colombo provided a convenient overflow base, with much better facilities for libertymen, but the port was shared with commercial traffic. Apart from the East Indies Fleet's ocean minesweepers, which were based there from the spring of 1945, Colombo tended to be used by ships arriving on (or passing through) the Station and by escorts.

The two Fleets in the Far East were saved further loss by the American use of the two atomic bombs. The East Indies Fleet led the reoccupation of Malaya and Singapore and supported the return of the French and Dutch to their former colonies, although they took no part in attempting to restore them to power. The BPF meanwhile reoccupied Hong Kong at the end of August and, with ships of all the Commonwealth and Allied Navies that had served under Admiral Fraser, had earned its right to be represented in the surrender ceremonies in Tokyo Bay in September.

The ceremonies did not mark the end of the two Fleets' work. In the Pacific theatre, all the large ships took part in the task of transporting the tens of thousands of returning allied prisoners of war and internees (RAPWI) from camps in Japan and China, a mission of mercy that lasted until the end of the year. The East Indies Fleet undertook RAPWI missions in South-East Asia and was then given the task of assisting the return of Dutch and French forces to their colonies, a payment for services rendered that cost British lives. It is improbable that these activities will ever be commemorated, but for those who took part, and did not return home until the greater part of a year after the return of peace in the European theatre, the services they rendered after the 'end' of the war were as important as their contribution to victory.

Table 9.2   The East Indies Fleet, VJ-Day, 1945

	East Indies Fleet	*Allocated*	*Passage to BPF*
Light Carriers	—	—	1
Escort Carriers	12	13	—
Battleships	2	2	—
Cruisers	7	8	2
Destroyers	16	24	3
Escort Destroyers	4	20	2
Sloops & Frigates	30	55	6

The BPF moved its base to Hong Kong in early 1946, relieving the financial burden on Australia. There was, understandably, less rejoicing at the departure than there had been for the original arrival and the many returns. Fifty years on, the memory of their time in Australia brings a wistful look to every RN veteran. A BPF pilot once described this time at Schofields as the antithesis of war— 95 per cent excitement and five per cent recuperation. It was not an uncommon experience, for the people of Fremantle, Melbourne, Brisbane and Sydney had brought a new dimension to total war—total hospitality.

10
'Something peculiar to themselves': The social background of the Navy's officers in World War II

Jason Sears

What types of people helped create and shape the RAN? Where did they come from? Was it truly an Australian Navy? Was the RAN representative of all Australians or only of a certain class or social group?

In July 1989 an Australian Naval History Seminar was conducted at the Australian Defence Force Academy in Canberra. In the introduction to the proceedings of that conference, the editors noted that there were 'yawning gaps in the historiography of the RAN' and that 'no attempt was made to approach naval social history simply because very little study of these matters is yet in hand in Australia.'[1]

In contrast to the Australian experience, the area of naval social history has achieved much international attention in recent years with works by McKee on the USN between 1794 and 1815, by Zimmerman on the social background of the RCN during World War II, and a sociological study of German U-boat crews by Mulligan.[2] Much more work has been done, and is in progress internationally, but we in Australia have sadly neglected an analytical approach to the social history of our Navy.

World War II was an important period in the social history of the RAN. The pre-war regulations, training, discipline and general efficiency of the RAN had been established on the British model. The RAN's senior officers were British, and there was a continuous interchange of officers, petty officers and men between the two navies. Australia recognised that it might be necessary in war to transfer control of the squadron, or individual ships, to the Admiralty.[3] In effect, the RAN was a squadron of the British Empire's navy.

George Hermon Gill believed, however, that World War II brought about great changes in the RAN. First, there was a large increase in the size of the RAN. In 1939 there were only 430 officers and 5010 ratings on the active list. With Reserve forces added, it was possible to more than double the Navy's strength to over 10 000 personnel at the start of the war. By the end of the war the Navy's

*1941 entry into the RANC with College officers and the Director of Studies. In mid-1940 in the first of the wartime applications, some 800 12–13-year-old boys attempted to join the RANC. The majority of the sixteen successful candidates came from state schools, and had fathers who had served in the ranks of either the British or Australian Army during World War I. One was the son of an ex-*Tingara *boy, while at the time of entry three fathers were officers in either the wartime RAAF, regular Army or CMF. (E.V. Stevens)*

strength had grown almost fourfold. Secondly, and most importantly, the majority of these personnel were Australians—products of the RANC and Flinders Naval Depot. This was in contrast to World War I when 20 per cent of the officers and sailors in the RAN were actually on loan from the RN.[4]

Unfortunately, there is no space to discuss every one of the 36 257 mobilised personnel serving in the RAN at the end of the war or the others who died or were discharged during the war years. The bulk of this study is limited to the officers for two reasons. The first is the crucial role played by officers in developing the young navy. As McKee wrote of the USN, seamen and petty officers came and went with enlistments, while history had demonstrated that a navy could have fine ships and establishments but that all of these counted for little without good officers.[5] The second reason is a more practical consideration. Clearly, there were far fewer officers than sailors and so the task of constructing a database and obtaining a statistically significant sample was made simpler by limiting the size of the study.

The primary source of the statistics used here are the 'Record of Service' cards held in Australian Archives and Navy Office. By sampling these, a statistical profile of the seaman officers who served in the RAN during World War II has been developed. A total of 274 records were randomly selected— 147 of the officers who entered the Navy through the RANC, 106 members of the executive branch of the RANVR, and 21 members of the RANR (Seagoing) (RANR(S)). Overall, the records of seven per cent of the officers who served in the RAN during the war were examined.

Place of birth

The first question considered was where had the officers of the RAN come from? As the service cards did not record where each person lived at the time he joined, these figures are based on the place of birth.

From Table 10.1 it is clear that the country of birth of the Navy's officers was very similar to the national average. The only figure that might be unusual is that for RANC entries with 93 per cent of them born in Australia compared to the national average of 85 per cent.

One issue of some importance when the Naval College was being established was to ensure that each state was fairly represented in the annual intakes. Initially, a quota system was used to select candidates. After only two years this system disappeared and the most suitable candidates were selected in order of merit regardless of state of residence.[6]

Table 10.2 shows that despite the removal of the quota system, there was roughly proportional representation between the officers born in each of the states compared to that state's total population. One significant discrepancy exists with the RANR(S) officers with 61 per cent of them having been born in NSW. This could have reflected the concentration of the Australian Fleet and much of the nation's merchant marine around Sydney which would have made it convenient for people from there to become officers in the RANR(S). Another point of significance is that the proportion of Tasmanians who joined as naval officers was almost twice as great as the national average.

Of great interest to Australian historians is the dichotomy between metropolitan areas and country regions. In 1939, 47 per cent of Australians lived in the cities and suburbs of Sydney, Melbourne, Brisbane, Adelaide, Perth and Hobart, yet 64 per cent of the Navy's officers born in Australia came from these areas.

The metropolitan bias in naval enlistment figures may be related to the fact that those who joined the Navy usually had some experience of the ocean whether it be through profession, recreation or simply the region of the country they came from. Indeed, as Table 10.3 shows, the great majority of the Navy's officers had

Table 10.1 Country of birth

Type of entry	Born in Australia (%)	Born in Britain (%)	Born elsewhere (%)
RANC	93	5	2
RANVR	82	12	6
RANR(S)	86	5	9
National average	85	12	3

Table 10.2 State of birth of those born in Australia

Type of entry	NSW (%)	VIC (%)	QLD (%)	SA (%)	WA (%)	TAS (%)
RANC	35	29	12	8	12	4
RANVR	38	26	13	7	10	6
RANR(S)	61	22	11	–	–	6
National average	39	28	14	9	7	3

Table 10.3 Region of birth

Type of entry	Born coastal Australia (%)	Born inland Australia (%)
RANC	80	20
RANVR	91	9
RANR(S)	94	6

been born in the coastal regions and Reserve officers were even more likely to have been born on the coast.

The large number of officers born on the coast mirrors the fact that most Australians happen to have been born in the nation's coastal regions.[7] The higher proportion of reserves born on the coast reflected the RAN's recruiting policies. The Navy, quite understandably, initially directed their officer recruiting in the war towards men between 30 and 40 years of age with boating or yachting experience. Subject to passing a selection board and physical test, these men would be granted direct commissions into the RANVR. The system changed as the war progressed and such qualified men were no longer available. Younger, less experienced men would be recruited as 'Ordinary Seamen Potential Officers' and spend about twelve months on the lower deck before sitting their selection boards for officer appointments.[8]

Age

War is often described as a young man's occupation and the RAN certainly took in its officers at a young age. From the time that the RANC opened in Geelong in 1913 until 1955 when the College was at Flinders Naval Depot, the major avenue of entry into the permanent RAN as an officer was to join the College as a 13-year-old. It was believed necessary to take in boys at such a young age as Australian schools were seen to promote a general atmosphere of independence and to form young men who later would not take kindly to naval discipline. Advocates of the system also argued that at thirteen, boys would absorb the necessary naval atmosphere and traditions and thus 'become imbued with officer-like qualities.'[9]

By the outbreak of war in 1939 the average age of RANC-trained officers in the Navy was 29. The youngest officers were thirteen and commencing their first year at the College while the oldest RANC-trained and serving officer was Captain Collins who was 40.

By the end of 1941, the average age of RANVR officers was 28.5 while the RANC average age remained remarkably steady—having fallen slightly to 28 years. These averages were to remain fairly steady throughout the war. It meant that the professional officers in the Navy had, on average, fifteen to sixteen years of experience behind them which they were able to pass on to their similarly aged colleagues in the Reserve forces. These average ages are remarkably similar to those in the RCN where in 1942 the average age of RCN officers was 29, and 28 years for RCNVR officers.[10]

The experience of the Australian Army was quite different. At the start of the war, the average age of the AIF's battalion commanders was 42.9. By 1945 their average age had fallen to 35.6.[11] The contrasting experiences of the two services served to demonstrate an essential difference between them. The Australian Military Forces (AMF) entered the war as a citizen force, supported by a tiny Permanent Military Force, unprepared for the following conflict. It grew rapidly, shedding older citizen officers who were worn out by the initial rigours of the war. Younger citizen officers moved upward fairly quickly as the citizen-based force continued its rapid growth. In contrast, the RAN had a relatively smooth mobilisation and quickly assumed its duties as part of the Empire Navy and later operated in the Pacific under the overall direction of the USN. By June 1945 only 40 413 personnel had enlisted in the RAN compared to 542 570 enlistments in the AMF by August 1943.[12] Consequently, the RAN remained a relatively stable force whose senior officers were nearly all Permanent naval force (PNF) personnel.

Education and class

Australians like to think of themselves as having a largely classless society. Many studies have shown, however, that this is not the case with occupation, wealth, income, education and place of residence usually being indications of a person's place in Australian society.[13] In her recent book, *Journeyings*, McCalman has described an Australia in the inter-war years that was divided by class and religion with the class divisions most evident in the education of its children.[14] Private education was very much part of the middle-class way of life in Australia. The connection between class and education, however, was not straightforward. There were great distinctions within both the state school systems and the private schools themselves. McCalman found that the children who attended the more exclusive private schools were generally the children of the upper—and middle—classes. However, some parents from the working and lower middle classes, aspiring to entry into the middle class for their children, would often send their children to such schools for short periods to be 'finished' and make the right social connections. The children at such private schools were told constantly that they were fortunate, privileged and special. They were children who may have been imbued with a sense of service but who nevertheless found it difficult to feel and relate to the mass of their fellow Australians in the working classes.[15] These children, particularly those who attended the corporate or independent schools represented at the Headmaster's Conference of Australia, were the children that the RAN targeted for recruitment into its officer class.

Officially, the RANC was open to every Australian boy of 'pure European descent' who was fit for entry. This fitness was determined by an academic exam, a searching series of physical tests and the recommendation of an interviewing panel who would select 'that special type which their own knowledge and experience associates with the title of "Naval Officer" '. No nomination was necessary and, unlike the British system, the whole cost of education at the College was borne by the Commonwealth and the cadet midshipmen were provided with free uniforms and a small wage.[16]

Unofficially, the system favoured boys who had a private school education. Indeed, the Navy actively targeted the private schools in its officer recruiting campaigns. As early as 1925 the Headmaster of the RANC, concerned about the number of boys the College had been receiving from 'humbler homes', had been writing personal letters to the Headmasters of the 'Great Public Schools' urging them to forget their 'snobbery' and send the 'right stuff' to the College.[17] In 1934, following a visit to Australia, Sir Maurice Hankey, the Secretary of the Committee of Imperial Defence wrote:

> So far as the Navy is concerned, I was informed that applicants for cadetships were not coming forward from what is usually spoken of as 'the officer class'. For example, applicants are not coming forward in any considerable numbers from the Australian Public Schools. 'Class consciousness' is probably far less marked in Australia than in the United Kingdom. Nevertheless it is probably inconvenient to find in the same ship one brother who is an officer in the wardroom mess and another who is a mess waiter in the wardroom—a condition which is stated to exist in one ship today. The Royal Navy is probably officered from a much wider class than was formerly the case, and in particular the facilities for promotion from the Lower Deck are much greater than in former times. Nevertheless, the bulk of the officers are still drawn from the professional classes, and, in the long run it will probably facilitate co-operation if the same is true of Australia.[18]

The Navy was careful to hide this bias in favour of private school boys from the government as evidenced by a letter from the Captain of the College to the ACNB in 1928 which stated that:

It appears undesirable to advertise the fact that officers from the College are lecturing on 'The Navy as a Career' as, although we know that it is the boys from such schools as I have quoted above (eg Cranbrook School, Sydney; St Peters College, Adelaide) that we want, questions might be asked as to why all the State Schools were being left out.[19]

It was claimed by Gill in the official history of the war that it was the democratic selection policies of the RAN (as compared to those in the RN) that provided the RAN with a range of officers from diverse backgrounds. Australian officers were seen to retain their individuality and variety of personality which made them better leaders of Australian sailors—who were typically seen as independent and resistant to authority (much like the stereotype of Australian soldiers and their officers).[20] Clearly, however, the Navy was not averse to going outside the general selection principles set down by the government.

Indeed, the democratic nature of the RAN's officers has been overstated. In 1939 78 per cent of Australian children were educated at state schools while only 22 per cent attended private schools.[21] However, 61 per cent of boys who entered the Naval College had been educated at private schools while only 39 per cent had attended a state school.[22] Of those who attended private schools, 59 per cent had attended one of the corporate or independent schools that the Navy viewed as 'GPS or first class'. Thus, a remarkable 36 per cent of the Navy's RANC-trained officers had attended one of the first-class independent schools. In contrast, despite having a higher entry age, the RMC, Duntroon, was only able to attract a slightly higher proportion of entrants from independent schools than from state schools in the 1920s while numbers from independent schools fell in the 1930s when prospects of a career in the Army were seen as poor.[23]

It is therefore likely that the majority of permanent RAN officers were from middle- and upper-class backgrounds. Those boys who did not come from such a background were soon shaped to the Navy's ideal for, as the Headmaster of the College had stressed in his letter to the GPS headmasters:

Believe me that I see to it that the leaven is applied from the top and that rough diamonds are cut to the pattern of the best leaders. Jervis Bay Cadets when they leave here are second to none in point of honour, manners and the graces which go to make a gentleman.[24]

Religion

Prior to World War II, and well beyond it, religion was a divisive force in Australian society. World War I had seen a renewed identification of the Protestant churches with Australian Imperial loyalty while during and after the war there had been accusations of Catholic disloyalty for opposing conscription and this, in the words of Roger Thompson, 'reinforced separatism between Catholics and Protestants'.[25]

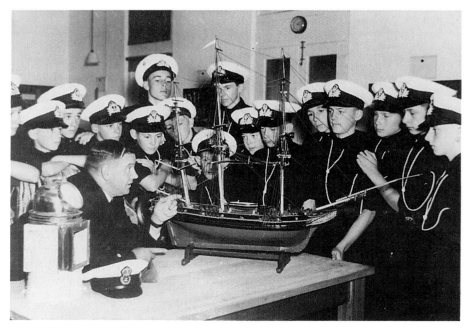

RANC 1941 entry at Seamanship instruction (the instructor was CPO Mackay who had first served as a boy seaman in the Boxer Rebellion and later during WWI). Two of the 1941 entry were discharged within a few months. Of the thirteen who graduated in August 1944 (two were Catholics): two were killed in naval aviation accidents as lieutenants, one died as a lieutenant-commander, two retired as commanders and three as captains, the last serving retired in 1982 as a rear-admiral. (E.V. Stevens)

No other service symbolised imperial loyalty more than the RAN[26] and this close connection between the Australian Navy and the British may well have discouraged Catholics from joining the RAN because Catholics were certainly under-represented in the ranks of the Navy's officers.

As is evident from Table 10.4, the RAN's officers were Christians, and Christians of the Protestant faith. Despite 22 per cent of Australians being Roman Catholics, only six per cent of the Navy's officers in World War II were. What is more surprising is that Reserve officers were even more likely to be Protestant than were their permanent counterparts. The reasons for this are not clear as the Catholic Church did not oppose Australia's participation in the war. It may have been that the top brass of the three services discouraged Catholics, and others, from becoming officers with their belief, in McCalman's words, that 'the urban working-class male might have had a larrikin's courage, but he was also danger-ous—he was sharp, disrespectful, sometimes criminal and more than likely to be a member of a trade union as well as a Catholic'.[27] None of these attributes were the 'right stuff' for naval officers.

Table 10.4 Religion

Type of entry	Church of England (%)	Presbyterian (%)	Methodist (%)	Baptist (%)	Church of Christ (%)	Roman Catholic (%)	Other (%)
RANC	68	20	2	1	1	8	–
RANVR	64	21	9	1	–	5	–
RANR(S)	66	22	11	–	–	–	–
National average	40	13	13	2	1	22	9

Catholics were also under-represented in the Army. Until the end of World War II, only 11 per cent of officers in the Permanent Military Forces who had entered through Duntroon were Catholic. While this was nearly twice the proportion that the Navy selected, it was still only half the proportion of Catholics in the total Australian population. Coulthard-Clark suggests that in the case of Duntroon, this had more to do with the working-class backgrounds of most Catholics than with their Irish (and therefore anti-British) backgrounds.[28] It is likely that both working-class background and anti-British sentiment discouraged and prevented many Catholics from joining the Navy.

Permanent and reserve officers

From this statistical sample of the RAN's seaman officers, it would appear that as a group they were not representative of Australian society in general. The typical Australian naval officer was a Protestant male of around 28-years of age. He had been born in one of Australia's capital cities and was more likely than not to have come from a privileged middle-class background. Few women were able to join the Navy and only then in limited numbers as members of the WRANS with highly limited career opportunities. Catholics were either not attracted to the RAN because of its strong Imperial ties or were rarely appointed by the Navy as officers due to their working-class backgrounds.

Surprisingly, there were few apparent differences in the social backgrounds of permanent and reserve naval officers. Then again, perhaps this really is not too unexpected. Entry into the RAN as an officer during World War II was highly competitive. As those who selected Reserve officers were senior permanent or ex-permanent officers themselves, they were always likely to continue past selection procedures and select young men whose character, background and beliefs were similar to their own. Little wonder then that McCalman found that the proportion of private school boys in the Navy and Air Force was higher than the national average with these young men also much more likely to hold commissions. Indeed, she determined that a man educated at Melbourne Grammar was five times more likely to gain a commission than the average serviceman, while even graduates from the school whose ex-students in her study were least

119

represented in the military, the Catholic Trinity College, were two and a half times more likely to become officers.[29]

Given their similar backgrounds, it is not surprising that Reserve officers in World War II generally learned quickly and fitted in well with their permanent RAN colleagues. Collins later wrote that he envied the many Reserve officers who, with so little sea training, were able to join a ship and be immediately at ease.[30]

There was, of course, a big learning curve for the new Reserve officers. One of them, Leggoe, described how most Reserve officers were required to learn on the job and received little formal naval training. It meant that they made mistakes but in time learned to 'earn their keep'.[31] Not everyone was so philosophical concerning the occasional mistakes made by Reserves learning new jobs under the stress of war. An able seaman recorded in his diary that:

> Permanent service officers, trained continuously from the age of 13 years, were the very best of their calling, equal to any Royal Navy opposite number . . . They were the very best of Australians . . . such appraisal could not be said of the many RANVR who coming from behind desks; bank tellers, accountants etc lacked those qualities engrained in the professional naval officer . . . the lower deck called them ninety day wonders . . . Some were excellent, most were better left ashore . . .[32]

The RANC-trained officers certainly had a wealth of experience behind them and a proud tradition of professionalism inherited from the RN. They had joined the Navy as thirteen-year-old boys, spent four years at the Naval College, six to twelve months in an Australian training cruiser and then another twelve to eighteen months in RN ships in European waters allowing the midshipmen to gain experience of a wide range of vessels from battleships to minesweepers. At the end of this period they would sit for seamanship examinations and, if they passed, be promoted to sub-lieutenant. The next twelve months would be spent training in RN shore establishments undertaking courses in subjects such as gunnery, navigation and torpedoes including a six-month period in the RN College at Greenwich. On successful completion of these courses and depending on how much 'time' had been gained during their training, the officers would be promoted to lieutenants some eight years after joining the College. As senior sub-lieutenants and lieutenants, the officers would join various RAN and RN ships to earn their watchkeeping tickets. By the time they were twenty-nine they would be newly promoted lieutenant-commanders with a wealth of seagoing experience. Some would have gained specialist qualifications in gunnery, navigation, torpedoes, communications, submarines, flying, surveying and so on. The products of this system were experienced, well but narrowly trained and highly professional naval officers.[33]

The influence that these RANC-trained officers were to have upon the RAN during World War II was critical. While the Navy grew from a permanent force of 5430 in 1939 to a peak strength of 36 976, the growth was not nearly as great as that of the Australian Army or Air Force or similar navies such as the RCN.

Indeed, the RCN grew from 3843 to over 95 000 personnel. These were truly citizen forces. Even at peak strength, officers of the permanent naval forces serving in the RAN made up 22 per cent of the RAN's total number of officers and permanent ratings made up 19 per cent of the total number of ratings.[34] As Frame, Goldrick and Jones have suggested:

> The RAN, unlike the Australian Army, was in large measure a permanent service which approached the challenges of a world conflict with as little modification of its standing organisation as possible. The ethos of the RAN came not so much from the citizen sailor, despite the remarkable contributions of Reservist and 'Hostilities Only' personnel during the major conflicts, but from the 13-year-old entry officers, the boy sailors of HMAS TINGIRA and the 'twelve year engagement men'.[35]

How then, in the complex hierarchical social system that made up the Navy, did these officers and their reserve colleagues relate to their subordinates—the lower deck who formed the bulk of naval personnel?

Officer–sailor relations

The answer to this question is not straightforward. Empirical data about officer–sailor relations is difficult to find and much of the evidence must therefore be anecdotal.

Lieutenant-Commander F.S. Holt joined the RANVR as an officer candidate with the rank of ordinary seaman in April 1941 via the 'Yachtsman's Scheme'. He spent a year on the lower deck of a RN ship before he was commissioned and by the end of the war was serving as the executive officer of the AMS HMAS *Gascoyne*. As a rating, he observed that the British officers considered themselves 'superior beings' and so when he gained his commission Holt consciously tried to bridge the gap between officers and ratings. While he was sure he gained some respect he discovered that 'naval tradition (symbolised by the officer's uniform) created some insuperable obstacles, as did also the constant work load it was my lot to perform which left no time to establish other than superficial relationships with the naval ratings'.[36] Given his experience in both the RN and the RAN, Holt believed that Australian sailors expected to be treated by their officers as intelligent individuals while British sailors would obey any order instantly. To give an Australian sailor a sharp order that did not make sense to him would lead to an attitude of resistance. Thus, as the ship's executive officer, Holt took the time to explain the purpose of any particular routine, exercise or order and would then receive cooperation. It also meant that constructive suggestions would be forthcoming from below.[37]

A different view of officer–sailor relations was given by an able seaman signalman in the PNF who served in HMAS *Vendetta* during the war. In his diary he noted that a 'gulf' existed between the lower deck and the wardroom which he described as a 'select club'. The rating wrote that while 'permanent naval officers were respected, few were liked' and that the sailors were always kept 'conscious of rank'. However, he also noted that the gulf between Australian ratings and Australian officers was less than that between the Australian sailors and RN officers whom he described as 'pigs'.[38]

The able seaman may have exaggerated how Australian sailors generally felt towards their RN officers but the belief that RN officers kept a greater distance between themselves and the lower deck than did Australian officers is a recurring theme in many memoirs and biographies of the period. Sir Henry Burrell, who was later to become CNS of the RAN from 1959 to 1962, wrote in his memoirs that on leaving the British cruiser HMS *Devonshire* the RN captain had taken special care to point out to him that he was 'too familiar with the sailors'—a criticism with which Burrell did not agree. He believed ships were more efficient when the officers and ratings were in closer touch.[39]

Conclusions

At the end of the war Admiral Sir Ragnar Colvin, RN wrote an obituary in response to the loss of RAN Captains Waller, Burnett and Getting. It read, in part:

> No finer sailors ever trod the deck. To one who has known them and worked with them there was something out of the ordinary about these sailors of the RAN. Coming from the Australian Naval College they worked and trained for years on their own and with the Royal Navy but they were never mere copyists. They assimilated the knowledge and traditions of the older service, but blended with it something peculiar to themselves and the result was unmistakable and unmistakably good.[40]

Colvin was correct when he wrote that the Australians were 'peculiar to themselves' in the sense that they were a blend of Australian character and RN training. The RAN certainly had close ties to the RN. The typical naval officer, both permanent and reserve, could be described as a middle-class, Protestant male who more often than not had received a privileged private school education. His background would generally have been little different from the typical RN naval officer's that Hankey described as coming from the professional classes.

That said, successive Australian governments were committed to making positions in the RAN available to all Australians. Indeed, some 40 per cent of RAN officers had come from humbler backgrounds although they were then educated and trained in the 'right stuff' by the Navy. By World War II, the great majority of RAN officers had been born and educated in Australia. Before being sent to Britain to complete their naval training, permanent RAN officers were educated at an Australian naval college. Australian officers also appear to have had a greater empathy for those on the lower deck although a certain distance between officers and ratings remained. The service as a whole was disciplined, effective and cohesive throughout the war.

It is unlikely, however, that the war had a particularly democratising effect on the RAN. It was not a citizen force in the sense that the Australian Army and the RCN were. Its officers were less representative of Australian society generally than were their counterparts in the AMF. Its numbers, particularly in the more senior ranks and positions, included a significant proportion of permanent personnel and long-time reservists as well as some RN personnel on loan. In this way, perhaps more than any other, the RAN was something peculiar to itself. By the end of World War II it was not seen as typical of the Australian experience of war—most Australians related to the Army 'digger's' experience of war.[41] The Navy was to remain the little-known 'silent service'.

11
Willing volunteers, resisting society, reluctant Navy: The troubled first years of the Women's Royal Australian Naval Service

Kathryn Spurling

In Australia, immigration patterns, geographic features and a particular historical period combined to create a virulently male-dominated society. This was particularly apparent in the armed services. Australia was a country where the ANZAC legend was revered—the legend was sacred and the myth was masculine. Unlike the governments of countries such as the United States and the United Kingdom which accepted women for service in the defence forces as early as 1917, the Australian Government resisted such policy. As the war clouds gathered over Europe for another generation, large numbers of Australian women began to mobilise themselves into paramilitary organisations. Their resolve and determination demonstrated that Australian women were ready to participate actively in the war effort. Initially 'ridiculed' these paramilitary organisations were to provide a valuable, trained nucleus when the Australian Government had no option but to accept female volunteers.

The two organisations most important to the formation of the Women's Royal Australian Naval Service (WRANS) were the Women's Reserve Emergency Naval Service (WRENS), later known as the WNS, and the Women's Emergency Signal Corps (WESC). Director of the WNS was Lillian Cooke. She badgered the RAN to provide instructors and by the end of 1940 WNS volunteers had gained access to RAN depots and hospitals.

Florence Violet Mackenzie, known to all as 'Mrs Mac', formed the WESC with the strong conviction that in communications 'female operators would demonstrate a competence equal to if not superior to male operators'. While she battled for official recognition she designed a 'model arm' which simplified the teaching of Morse code and by June 1940 sixty members of the WESC were qualified instructors. Over the next year some 3500 RAAF recruits received their initial Morse code instruction at WESC headquarters and the RAAF had commenced enlistment of WESC personnel for the Women's Auxiliary Australian Air Force (WAAAF).

Troubled by a severe shortage of wireless operators the RAN agreed to the enrolment of fourteen WESC signallers to work alongside RAN personnel at HMAS *Harman* from 21 April 1941. Still dressed in their bottle-green WESC uniforms the signallers were placed on call 24-hours a day in line with naval ratings and accommodated in two cottages on the *Harman* perimeter. They remained 'civilian'. Between female volunteers and naval service stood one of the most influential of Australian politicians, William Morris Hughes. In a letter to the acting Prime Minister dated 2 April 1941, the 78-year-old Minister for the Navy wrote, 'In my opinion the employment of females in the navy is undesirable'.

On 29 July 1941 the Australian War Cabinet consented to the establishment of the Australian Women's Army Service (AWAS). The Minister for the Army had argued that the formation of the AWAS would result in the release of men for fighting units and female volunteers would be less expensive. No such case in favour was put by the then Minister for the Navy, Norman Makin. There remained within the offices of the Department of the Navy strong resistance to the recruitment of women. The female signallers employed by the RAN continued in their semi-official status, denied the recognition they so badly desired.

It was a female volunteer signaller, Jess Prain, who in December 1941 dispatched to all ships from the *Harman* transmitting station the message that Australia was at war with Japan. At the tri-service conference convened to discuss service conditions for the women's auxiliary services a month later, the AWAS was represented by its controller, Sybil Irving, and Wing-Commander Claire Stephenson represented the WAAAF. The 26 women employed with the RAN were represented by Commander Jack Newman.

At the same time, however, the RAN continued to accept surreptitiously the employment of female volunteers. Members of the WNS worked in the supply and pay offices at Garden Island, paid 2s 6d per day by the Commonwealth Public Service. Members of the Voluntary National Emergency Service Ambulance Drivers operated the service ambulance out of HMAS *Rushcutter*, the ambulance itself provided from funds raised by members.

Other female volunteers committed many hours each week to RAN-supported organisations while they remained unpaid and unacknowledged. One such organisation was the Minewatchers, an organisation through which women were trained to carry out the duties associated with the early detection of enemy submarines and aircraft. In Queensland the Minewatcher organisation was under the control of Captain E.P. Thomas.

Volunteers were 'sworn to absolute secrecy' and assigned two to a post. Minewatcher posts along the Brisbane River resembled bunkers, being constructed of reinforced concrete $8 \times 8 \times 6$ feet in area with a back entrance and a covered slit window in the front. Each shelter contained a bunk, a blanket, a

WRANS at the Balmoral Depot marching to the parade ground for morning Divisions, 1942. Joan Streeter in the middle front rank would go on to be Director WRANS in peacetime service. (K. Spurling)

small Primus stove and a direct telephone line to naval headquarters. There was no electricity or ablution facilities.

Joy Winnett was a secretary with a legal firm and at 5.30 each afternoon she would change into her Minewatcher uniform and travel by public transport to begin the 6pm–6am duty. She would set up the bearing plate in the bunker's front slit window and await the vessels that would drop smoke bombs for minewatcher tracer practice. Each night an RAN truck would drop female volunteers at Pinkenba at the mouth of the Brisbane River. Their responsibility included making reports on shipping, taking note of every ship that entered the Brisbane River and how close to the shoreline each vessel passed.

RAN written instructions provided to members of the Minewatchers suggested how vital a service the organisation was performing and accepted that the conduct of such duties involved an element of danger. Instruction number five of the information sheet written by Lieutenant-Commander V.M. Bowden included the following:

> What to do if the post is machine gunned: Crouch down on the floor as low as possible and right up against the front wall. In this position it is absolutely impossible to be hit by a machine-gun bullet.

To this day the RAN has not admitted to the existence of the Minewatchers.

Japanese forces advanced rapidly towards Australia. The surrender of Singapore on 15 February 1942 meant an end to any remaining delusions of safety held by the Australian people. Prime Minister Curtin announced there would be a complete mobilisation of all Australian resources, human and material. But the complete mobilisation of women continued to be resisted by a social system that excluded women from many professions. With the formation of the AWAS came the Melbourne *Argus*' headline 'Women's army policy not to replace men'. Throughout the war female volunteers received approximately 66 per cent of the male pay rate or, if under 21 years of age, 57 per cent.

1942 was a horrific year for the RAN, Australia's sea defence capacity being severely jeopardised with the loss of many ships and men. When survivors from HMAS *Canberra* returned to Sydney, RAN authorities requested assistance from the WNS. Lorna Nagrint recalled: 'We were there handing out razor blades, cap tallies, etc. when one battered hero sighted us and said "Gawd, bloody women"'.

The Women's Royal Australian Naval Service, 1942–45

The sailor's reaction was one being repeated in the highest echelons of the RAN, the only Australian defence force yet to enlist women into its ranks. On 24 July 1942 a Navy Office conference finally moved to alter Australian naval tradition when it was agreed that 580 female volunteers would be recruited, of whom 280 would be telegraphists. In September the ACNB simply informed commanding officers throughout Australia that:

> It has been decided that the Women's Royal Australian Naval Service (WRANS) shall from 1 October 1942 consist of personnel enlisted for service under the Naval Defence Act 1910–1934 as members of the Commonwealth Naval Forces.

Signallers at *Harman* were the first offered enlistment, with Frances Provan becoming WRAN no. 1. Further enlistment progressed steadily but without haste. Despite a government instruction in July that 1000 WRANS be inducted by November 1942, only 332 recruits were accepted by this date—the RAN continued to resist. Volunteers accepted for service discovered an organisation totally uncomfortable with the circumstances in which it had been placed.

During the earliest stages of the WRANS, confusion, uncertainty and awkwardness were evidenced. Volunteers were assured they would enter in the 'near future' but many would find the 'near future' meant many months of waiting. Victoria's Betty Smart waited fourteen months before she was instructed to join the Flinders Naval Depot. Many prospective recruits found the duration between acceptance for the WRANS and actual call-up unacceptable and chose instead to enter the AWAS or WAAAF. Volunteers already fully trained as signallers recall a period which was 'a very frustrating period, a wasteful non-utilisation of our would be war effort'. Following the appearance of a WRANS recruiting advertisement in a Townsville newspaper, Molly Smith presented herself at the gates of HMAS *Magnetic* but was informed by RAN authorities 'that no provisions as yet had been made for the acceptance of female recruits'. Molly persevered and entered as a WRAN writer only to find an 'Administration totally unprepared for us, no uniforms, no separate messing arrangements had been made and we were not allowed to use the RAN mess'.

Although the formation of the WRANS had been in the organisational stages for some years, naval issue for the first female entries consisted of a suitcase, a white armband with the blue lettering WRANS, a pair of sandshoes and a gas mask. The first volunteer signaller enlisted in Melbourne to join *Harman* was told to wear her WESC uniform. Not being a member of this Sydney-based organisation she wore the only uniform she had, her old girl guide uniform. At HMAS *Moreton* the first uniform issue was winter rig and in the Brisbane summer the new WRAN ratings 'boiled' in their navy serge. In other centres such as Adelaide's HMAS *Torrens*, it would be many weeks after enlistment before uniform issue.

Unlike their male counterparts, female entries were not sent to a centralised naval training establishment, with local facilities used instead. With no guidelines finalised for female recruit training the first intakes of WRANS received courses containing many of the elements in the male recruit course. Along with the lectures on 'naval discipline and customs', were lectures titled 'parts of ship', 'anchors and cables', 'torpedoes and depth charges' and practical demonstrations on 'rigging', 'hammock slinging and lashing' and 'care for explosives'. Although members of the first general intake did not realise the significance of such training, they had been given a rare insight into the nautical aspects of the service with which they were now affiliated. Rare, because for ensuing intakes of WRAN recruits, not only during the war years but for the generations of WRANS who would follow them in the 1950s, 1960s and 1970s, recruit course training would be devoid of any material pertaining to a seafaring navy.

The first intake of sixteen WRANS in South Australia occurred on Trafalgar Day 1942. The new recruits received two and a half weeks training at the South Australian naval depot at Birkenhead. This training was to prepare them for positions as clerks, typists, transport drivers, mess stewardesses and stores assistants. Connie Foxton who joined as a visual signaller discovered, 'Our course was much shorter than that which the sailors did, and we had to master the practical part of the course faster'.

In March 1943, two years after the RAN had commenced employing female telegraphists at *Harman*, the Governor-General of Australia, Lord Gowrie, signed statutory rule no. 67 which amended the *Naval Defence Act* to include the WRANS.

Throughout Australia, female volunteers were motivated to enlist for naval service for the same reasons their male counterparts were; 'The sense of adventure, the glamour of the uniform and the feeling of helping to win the war'. Australian men and women alike realised that, if Australia was to survive the war, it would involve an unprecedented 'all in' effort. Nonetheless while it was generally expected that able-bodied young men should enter the defence forces, there remained an unwillingness within Australian society to expect the same commitment from able-bodied young women.

The advertising and editorial content of the Australian press helped to perpetuate this ambiguity. The media play an important role within society, providing ideological interpretation, and integrating preferred meanings from the overall culture to set 'acceptable' behaviour patterns. In the early 1940s the printed press continued to portray women's primary concerns as the home and family. Just as the media had been patronising and condescending towards the female paramilitary organisations, women in the armed forces were depicted for their novelty value, rather than as a serious alternative to an all-male defence of the country. Servicewomen were posed in delicate, clean, non-active poses, ones often unrelated to their duties. In cartoons WRANS personnel were portrayed as either leggy Betty Grable pin-up types complaining, 'I just can't get used to saluting him, kissing him and then having to salute him again', or the less attractive, squat, overweight, bespectacled WRAN saying, 'I joined for the travel, sport, adventure and as an alternative to lifelong spinsterhood'. Only as the war endured and the size of the women's auxiliaries increased did an Australian press, skilled in domesticating the female, shift ground and for a brief period take a more congratulatory and less hostile stance.

Many female volunteers found their conviction to enlist in the WRANS severely challenged by social and family dissension. June Jorgenson's family's naval tradition could be traced back to the sailor who carried Captain Cook ashore at Botany Bay but her family interpreted this tradition in purely male terms and her parents refused to sign the consent forms. As a consequence, June was unable to enlist as a WRAN writer until her twenty-first birthday. Heather Dunshea, a WESC trained wireless telegraphist, waited until the day of departure before telling her parents of her WRANS enlistment: 'My father told me that I had put myself in the category of camp follower and was quite disgusted.' Monica Palmer, too, would always remember her father's farewell comments: 'His fatherly advice was don't get pregnant you won't be welcomed home and please don't marry an American.'

The ACNB continued to regard the WRANS as a stop-gap measure, and the lack of any administrative or financial long-term commitment hampered service expansion. RAN rather than government policy continued to specify that vacancies for WRANS be filled where possible by women from the particular home port where the manpower shortages existed and that these recruits continue to reside in their parental homes, travelling to duty on public transport. During 1942 and 1943 only a small number of WRANS from the communication branch were sent interstate.

The advantages to the RAN of such a policy were numerous. It was inconceivable during the early 1940s that RAN messing arrangements and quarters be shared by male and female personnel alike. WRANS residing in the parental home absolved the RAN of the responsibility for care and discipline of female personnel. A policy of nationwide transfer of female volunteers and a centralised scheme of training for female recruits required the RAN to commit itself to the development of the WRANS rather than simply agree to the requirement for a corps of uniformed civilians.

Unlike its Army and Air Force counterparts the Navy was reluctant to commission female volunteers. The inclusion of the WRANS under the *Naval Defence Act* in early 1943 left the ACNB no further option but the appointment of a female administrator although they delayed until October the advertising for the position of 'First Officer—WRANS'. The selected candidate was Annette Oldfield and following her briefing with the commanding officers of other Women's Auxiliary Services, First Officer Oldfield commenced a tour to visit members of the service she now headed.

WRAN Mary Butler was appointed to act as First Officer Oldfield's driver during the director's visit to Adelaide shortly before Christmas. Mary was impressed with the 'confident and thorough' woman who questioned her on all aspects of her naval duties. When WRAN Butler reported for day two of the director's visit she found that Oldfield had been recalled to Navy Office and her resignation requested. The Naval Board had demonstrated a marked reluctance to agree to the appointment of female officers, and the first experiment with such an appointment had ended in public intrigue and discomfiture. Although there had been other applicants for the position of director, no further female officer appointments were made until the end of February 1943. The appointment of another Director WRANS was not officially promulgated until 16 January 1945.

The first WRANS officer training course commenced at the Flinders Naval Training Depot on 18 January 1943. The sixteen members of the first OTC came with diversified educational and employment histories. This rich background of human experience resulted in a strong officer nucleus which would make a most important contribution to the development of the WRANS. From the first course came the wartime director, Sheila McClemans, Margaret Curtis-Otter who was appointed by the Australian Government to supervise the re-establishment of the WRANS in 1950, and the first peacetime director, Blair Bowden.

All members successfully completed their training and were promoted to Third Officer WRANS. They were to be assigned WRANS' administration positions but the posting signal reflected the degree of the RAN's continuing unpreparedness. With the plans for WRANS' accommodation and administration blocks still incomplete the majority of the new WRANS officers were designated 'additional disposal' or 'temporarily attached'.

Throughout 1943 WRANS' facilities were slowly procured and constructed. Many WRANS' quarters such as those at Cairns, known as 'Homeleigh', were noticeably different and distant from RAN establishments. In major centres WRANS quarters were only large enough to house a portion of the female personnel enlisted, and, as a consequence, many service members continued to remain removed from the main vein of naval life. Quarters in Melbourne accommodated only 77 of the 126 WRANS and six WRANS officers employed. At *Penguin* the WRANS quarters catered for only 159 of the 275 personnel serving in the Sydney region. In July 1944, the condemned hospital, 'the Charlemount', was obtained to house some 100 WRANS personnel.

The first Queensland intake had taken place in November 1943, but it was thirteen months later before accommodation at *Moreton* was offered to half the number of WRANS personnel stationed in the Brisbane area. Quarters for members of the WRANS were not opened at Western Australia's HMAS *Leeuwin* until the last week in January 1945 although by then there were 163 ratings and eight WRANS officers in the area.

While the media showed servicewomen to be pampered, living conditions for many members of the WRANS were austere, but there were few complaints. According to one, 'Many of us found ourselves for the first time, having to adapt to living in a group and enjoyed the spirit of cooperation and camaraderie that existed'. For the WRANS as a service there was finally the opportunity to develop within its ranks a sense of unity.

During 1943 because of the lack of direction from Navy Office, individual RAN commanding officers were left to adapt and interpret as best they could what duties could be assigned female personnel; for this reason 1943 was the brightest year for diversification and opportunity. Dorothy Conaghty and Bonnie Johnston undertook a four-month cinema operator/dome teacher course. As it evolved this would be the longest training offered to any member of the Service. Other WRAN ratings found themselves drafted to the various degaussing ranges that dotted the Australian seaboard. An all too small number of female volunteers were given an opportunity to take to the water. A team of WRANS were employed as range markers on the rifle range at Flinders, assigned work that was physically demanding and dangerous. They were responsible for the armoury of pistols, rifles, Thomson, Bren and Owen guns, stripping, cleaning and reassembling the weapons. Theirs was the only profession where female volunteers worked directly with the tools of war and so was deemed too sensitive for public acknowledgment. Throughout Australia members of the WRANS endeavoured to make the most of their service conditions and demonstrated an abundance of industry and resourcefulness.

The first WRANS category to gain the acceptance of RAN authorities had been that of wireless operator. It had originally been decided that the conditions of service at port signal stations were too arduous for female volunteers, but when the opportunity arose members of the WRANS proved otherwise. In some of the outposts with the worst weather in Australia, WRANS stood on observation decks and served in underground bunkers throughout the day and night to detect, recognise and signal all varieties of shipping. By 1944 WRANS personnel made up 90 per cent of the complement of *Harman*, and Marion Stevens, the first WRAN

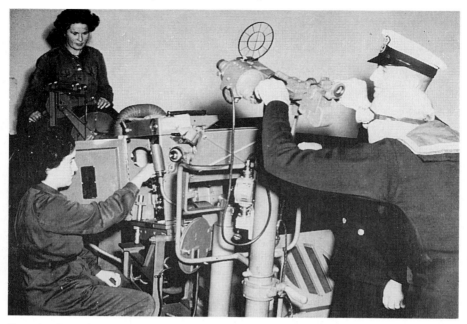

Dorothy Conaghty and Bonnie Johnston cinema operators/dome teachers at HMAS Cerberus. Their four-month course was the longest training offered to members of the WRANS. (K. Spurling)

to be promoted to the rank of chief, was placed in charge of the day-to-day operations at 'Molonglo', the high-speed communications satellite station.

But by the beginning of 1944 the basic WRANS structure within the larger RAN framework had been established and new RAN restrictions resulted in much less expansion and diversification. Whereas WRANS personnel were restricted to 27 categories, WAAAF personnel were listed in 53 different categories. Trade training was closed to female members of the Australian Navy. Unlike their Army and Air Force counterparts, trades like motor mechanic were not an option. In January of that year, the ACNB issued the instruction, 'It is not the intention to recruit any more WRANS'. The Service had always been awarded a very low profile and the RAN had never engaged in the recruiting campaigns of the other services. By March 1944, 49 000 women were members of the Australian Defence Force Auxiliaries. WRANS complement at that time consisted of a mere 1738 ratings and 58 officers.

Second Officer McClemans, who had been appointed to the Office of Naval Personnel as WRANS adviser, argued for a monthly service expansion of 50 ratings and ten officers to raise the WRANS establishment to 2338 enlisted personnel and 175 WRANS officers by the end of the year. As far as she was concerned, requests for WRANS personnel continued to exceed induction and the Service could expand to meet the demand. There was strong support for such

Range watchers at Cerberus. *These were the only WRANS to handle weapons during the war. (K. Spurling)*

an expansion from Allied Fleet Headquarters throughout Australia and neighbouring areas and General MacArthur had written requesting more WRANS personnel at Supreme Allied Headquarters. McClemans' proposal was rejected by the Naval Board. During 1944 and 1945 members of the United States Women's Auxiliary Services, the Women's Royal Naval Service and the Women's Royal New Zealand Naval Service arrived to relieve staff shortages at fleet bases in Australia.

The lack of provision for promotion was synonymous with the WRANS' temporary status but it was also synonymous with gender-related biases and beliefs. Women were not viewed to have the 'natural' traits necessary for leadership because of the prevailing stereotypical image of femininity. At a defence conference in 1942 it was decided that, 'There was likely to be considerable resentment if men were required to submit to discipline or take instructions from women members'. In some WRANS categories official promotion criteria was not promulgated until three years after initial intakes to that occupation. In some categories promotion provisions were never established. In July 1945 the ACNB established, 'A roster of advancement for WRANS on a fleet numbers basis'. This ruling ensured that the number of WRANS' higher rates would not exceed a small percentage of male higher rates.

The RAN maintained a reluctance to admit women to officer rank and to promote accordingly. In June of 1945, officers made up 10.2 per cent of total

RAN establishment, while in the WRANS the ratio was 4.3 per cent. When the manpower shortage necessitated that WRANS officers be appointed to RAN specialist positions, the WRANS officers concerned found promotion difficult to achieve. Female personnel could not serve at sea, and promotion was for those who had.

Members of the AWAS and WAAAF served in the Middle East, New Guinea and Pacific Areas; naval policy maintained that members of the WRANS be restricted to the safest naval establishments and none served overseas. Furthermore in what could be described only as a public relations exercise WRANS personnel were not allowed to serve in the forward area, Darwin, until June 1945, two months before the war with Japan ceased.

Conclusions

It took the largest threat to face the country before Australian tradition was broken with the ranks of the Defence Forces opened to female volunteers. The Australian War Cabinet, having set the guidelines for the conditions of service of members of the Women's Auxiliary Services in 1942, left the interpretation of such guidelines to its representatives on the individual service boards. The development of the WRANS was inhibited by the very conservative beliefs held by senior RAN administrators. Of the three service boards the ACNB imposed the most stringent limitations on the service opportunities of its female members. The WRANS was the last Women's Auxiliary Service formed, the last officially to enlist volunteers and the last women's service to appoint officers. Throughout World War II the WRANS were allowed to maintain the smallest number of volunteers, permitted to enter fewer service occupations than members of the AWAS and WAAAF and offered few opportunities for transfer. The underlying criteria for the selection of particular categories for members of the WRANS evolved not from the individual qualities and capabilities of the female volunteers but how their gender was perceived in society as a whole and by the RAN in particular. The very female nature of members of the WRANS nullified their position within the RAN. Naval life evolved around the sea, and the issue of female volunteers was fundamentally alien to the RAN's tradition of seafaring and naval warfare.

12
Vice-Admiral Sir John Augustine Collins, KBE, CB, RAN

A.W. Grazebrook

John Augustine Collins was born in Tasmania in 1899, the youngest son of a merchant navy doctor, who died before he was born. John's was a large family, to some of whom at least he remained close for many years.

Collins was a member of the first class of 1913 at the RAN College, where he was recognised as one of several cadets with great potential. He went to sea in the Grand Fleet battleship HMS *Canada* in 1917. After the war Collins served almost alternately with the RN (where he specialised in gunnery) and at home. In this well-planned succession of appointments he developed the balance of professional capabilities to fit him for senior posts ashore and afloat. His first command was a destroyer.

After a spell in the British Admiralty Naval Staff Plans Division handling local defence of naval ports, he became executive officer of the new cruiser HMAS *Sydney*. Here he had his share of bad luck, not the least of which was his delightful but imprudently humorous Captain, J.U.P. Fitzgerald. Although much liked by his ship's company, Fitzgerald appeared to his superiors to take professional naval matters insufficiently seriously. *Sydney*, which was detained in the Mediterranean during the Abyssinian crisis, was not well thought of by the commander of the cruiser squadron, Vice-Admiral Horton.[1] Later, Collins was to recount that this first *Sydney* commission gave him his first grey hairs.

In general, these preparatory years were good. The only gap was that there was little or no involvement with the merchant navy (from which Collins would have benefited immensely in Java in 1942).

When he was 31 Collins married Phyllis McLauchlan, from a moderately well-to-do Sydney family. The wealth helped because, in those days, when there was no such thing as a married accompanied billet, RAN officers struggled to meet their family and professional financial obligations.

On 3 September 1939 Captain Collins was serving in Navy Office in Melbourne as Assistant Chief of Naval Staff (ACNS). For a time prior to the war, he held the joint appointment of Director of Naval Intelligence, but in this he was replaced by classmate Commander Rupert Long. As ACNS, Collins played a major role in the preparation of the RAN for World War II. His involvement ranged from the new construction program to mobilisation.

In the former, Collins was involved in pressing the mobility advantages of maritime defence against the strongly continental defence views of some cabinet ministers, eliminating the pet projects of politicians (and his superior Admiral Colvin) in favour of practicable plans that would get the best value quickly. The pet projects ranged from Admiral Colvin's plan to buy a battleship from Britain to Billy Hughes' 'nests of torpedo boats'.

Nearly 40 years later, Collins was to recall that 'we were put off submarines by our failure with the J Boats' and to conclude that 'in the event the decision of the Australian Naval Board proved correct' in so far as their general balance of forces was concerned. For the first two years of the war the force of cruisers filled a very necessary role against German surface raiders and (with escorts and destroyers) supported the British forces overseas. After Japan's entry into the war, the RAN's cruisers and destroyers were well suited to the cruiser–destroyer actions in the South Pacific. The *Bathurst* class minesweeping corvettes (in the selection of which Captain Collins played a key role) were well suited to defending Australian waters against the Japanese submarine attacks when they came.[2] The problem lay in the shortage of seaborne air power. In the event this was provided by the USN.

At 0900 on 16 November 1939, at Fremantle, Captain Collins assumed command of the cruiser *Sydney*. General activity in all aspects of naval affairs, and his perception at this very early stage of the war of some of the events to come, can be recognised from his Reports of Proceedings (ROP).

Collins' ROPs of the period were always very complete, with both specific detail, observations and conclusions. They were punctually dispatched. Clearly, Collins knew how to ensure that his ROPs were read, when the rather dry reports of other commanding officers tended to gather dust in the bottom of Navy Office in-trays. Comparing Collins' ROPs with those of his contemporary captains, it is difficult to avoid the conclusion that he was 'pushing his own barrow' a bit. In fairness, it must be said that the ACNB needed to know what life was like for RAN ships so far from home in the Mediterranean.

The day after he assumed command, Collins attended a meeting of the Local Defence Coordinating Committee and was 'greatly concerned by the inadequate state of readiness maintained by fortress Fremantle. There was nothing to prevent a darkened raider approaching Gage Roads by night and operating and laying mines at her leisure. Apparently, no searchlights or counter bombardment guns were manned'.[3] Shortly afterwards, Collins flew in *Sydney*'s aircraft to see the aerodrome at RAAF Pearce.

Sydney continued to operate on the Australia Station, escorting convoys and patrolling the approaches to Fremantle and elsewhere. This involved a good deal of sea time (in one month, 26 out of 30 days). In March 1940, Collins' recognition of the value of favourable publicity, understanding of the two sister Services and ability to work with the press was shown when he embarked four press representatives, fifteen RAAF and 24 Army officers and the Mayor of Fremantle, to witness a 6-inch and 4-inch gun shoot.

While at sea, Collins was ordered to sail to Colombo, and thence to Aden and the Mediterranean. *Sydney* arrived in Alexandria on 24 May and became an integral part of the British Mediterranean Fleet, where she continued to serve until January 1941. An early feature of *Sydney's* service was the sinking of the Italian destroyer *Espero* and subsequent rescue of survivors, which was not undertaken without risk.

The highlight and best known achievement of *Sydney's* service in the Mediterranean was the sinking of the Italian cruiser *Bartolomeo Colleoni* and the damaging of her sister ship *Giovanni Delle Bande Nere* off Crete in July 1940. This action has been covered in detail many times and suffice it to say that, on his own initiative, Collins in *Sydney*, with five British destroyers, engaged two Italian cruisers each of similar armament to but markedly faster than *Sydney*.

There is no denying that, when he ordered his force to turn towards the Italian cruisers without knowing whether they were 6-inch or 8-inch gunned ships, Collins took a risk in adopting Nelson's approach of 'engage the enemy more closely'. During the action, and knowing nothing beyond a signal saying that the small force was turning towards the enemy, Collins' CinC (Admiral Sir Andrew Cunningham) 'was on tenterhooks' at Alexandria.[4] However, the risk proved well judged. Collins was immediately made Companion of the Most Honourable Order of the Bath. His naval reputation was made, as was that of *Sydney* and the RAN, in World War II.

It should be remembered that, up to that time, Collins was not the only senior RAN officer serving in the Mediterranean under Vice-Admiral Light Forces, John Tovey. Tovey and 'all on his staff had tremendous admiration and liking for (Captain) H.M.L. Waller (in command of *Stuart* and the 10th Destroyer Flotilla)—he was quite unique and a wonderful character, whereas Collins was just one of the nine very able Cruiser Captains under Tovey's command and not so colourful as Waller, although still very highly thought of'.[5] Nevertheless, Collins' difficulties in *Sydney* in the Mediterranean in 1935–36, when Cunningham was a key flag officer in the Fleet, were now overridden by an undoubted success in battle.

The importance of the *Bartolomeo Colleoni* action should not be allowed to overshadow *Sydney's* other achievements during her six months in the Mediterranean. She participated more or less continuously in a succession of operations, ranging from fleet activities to anti-aircraft (AA) guard in Alexandria, where Collins experienced his first air attacks.

Sydney's activities in November 1940 are typical of those of cruisers at the time. She started the month at sea with the main Fleet, returned to Alexandria on the 2nd, fuelled, and left the next day for Port Said to embark Army personnel and stores for Suda Bay. Approaching Suda on the 6th, she launched her aircraft on an anti-submarine patrol and then entered harbour and disembarked her cargo. On the 7th she joined the Battle Fleet to cover a convoy to Malta. Thence she undertook a sweep through the Straits of Otranto, rejoining the Battle Fleet during a day of continuous air attacks. At 0600 on the 14th *Sydney* arrived at Alexandria, with air-raid warnings at 1900, 2215, 2300, 0001 and 0115.

After fuelling on the 15th, *Sydney* sailed for operations with troops and stores for Greece, arriving in Piraeus on the 16th, sailing again on the 17th for convoy operations and patrols in the Aegean. *Sydney* returned to Alexandria on the 20th. She sailed again on the 23rd to join the Battle Fleet with a convoy for Crete. Without returning to Alexandria, she was detached with HM Ships *Eagle*, *Berwick* and six destroyers for an air attack on Tripoli, followed by covering a convoy to Malta. She returned to Alexandria at 1430 on 29 November, becoming AA guard ship.[6]

Sydney's service was not exceptional among the ships of the Mediterranean Fleet. However, it was very different and very demanding for Collins, compared with the long months of boredom and uneventful periods at sea in the Grand Fleet battleship *Canada* in 1917–18. At sea the ship's company were in two watches, all hands at their quarters during the night and all hands closed up for 70 minutes at dawn and dusk. On return to harbour, long hours were spent loading stores, ammunitioning, boiler cleaning, etc. Even then, AA guns were manned all night. (These figures are doubted by some officers who were serving then. However, the figures are taken from Collins' ROPs.)

In spite of all this work, always conscious of the need to highlight his country's presence, Collins gave receptions and other official entertainment. Thus in Piraeus he gave a lunch for Greek Naval Officers, the British Minister and others. In Alexandria, after the *Bartolomeo Colleoni* sinking, Collins gave an 'At Home' to the senior officers of the Fleet and Captains of HMA Ships present.

When *Sydney* returned to Sydney in February 1941, Collins and the rest of his ship's company had experienced a very different type of war to that of their contemporaries in cruisers patrolling the broad oceans against surface raiders. Collins had experienced the long periods of high degrees of readiness against submarine and air attack for which others were unprepared when Japan entered the war. Collins had learned to maintain his ship's company's alertness in these circumstances. Most of his contemporaries had not.

Collins remained in command of *Sydney* for three months after the ship's return to Australia. During that period, he took Admiral Colvin and a small staff to a conference in Singapore. As his ROP shows, Collins was unimpressed with the naval readiness at Singapore.

During the conference it was agreed that Collins would be appointed (after his relief in *Sydney*) Australian naval representative to Vice-Admiral Sir Geoffrey Layton, CinC China, at Singapore. Collins took up his new post on 17 June

1941.[7] The lack of consciousness at Singapore of impending Japanese attack, and just what that would mean, is exemplified by the fact that even Collins, with his experience of war in the Mediterranean where no one was safe wherever you were, took his wife to Singapore. On arrival, they had to wait while new senior officers' married quarters were built.[8]

Collins' combination of professional knowledge, practical war experience, pleasant personality and diplomatic skills was to prove well suited to his new post. Using his experience in the Admiralty's Plans Division and as ACNS in Melbourne, Collins went to work developing plans for joint operations with the Dutch Navy (at Batavia in what is now Indonesia) and the USN's Asiatic Fleet based in the Philippines. Collins was closely involved in requests to London for the reinforcements that were so clearly needed. In these days of reinterpreting history to the disadvantage of Britain, it is well to repeat the view of this very well-placed senior Australian officer writing in his autobiography some years later:

> Dispatches were sent to London asking for reinforcements but, with commitments in the UK, North Africa and Russia to meet, the wherewithal was just not available. Remember there was no certainty that Japan would declare war, whereas the European war was a grim reality.[9]

In Singapore Collins worked on PLENAPS (Plans for the Employment of Naval and Air Forces of the Associated Powers). These plans were in force by the time Japan attacked and involved a high degree of cooperation between the nations that later became allies. PLENAPS was predicated on a relief force arriving from Europe within 90 days.[10]

Collins got on well with Admiral Layton, but in a controversial change the latter was relieved by Admiral Phillips just before Japan entered the war. Phillips brought his own Chief of Staff and Captain of the Fleet, but Collins remained in his position. In spite of the fact that it was the agreed plan with the Allies, Collins was unable to persuade Phillips' staff to take PLENAPS seriously.

Phillips was soon to lose his life in the sinking of his flagship, HMS *Prince of Wales*. Collins was in the War Room at Singapore arranging tugs to tow the reportedly damaged ships and 'like the rest of the world, was stunned when the signal came saying both capital ships had been sunk'.[11]

This relatively short biographical chapter is not the time to re-examine the action in detail. Collins, ashore in the War Room working for Phillips' Chief of Staff, Admiral Palliser, did not even know of the tactical decisions made afloat by the CinC. Therefore, it is noteworthy that Collins was not as condemnatory of Phillips as are a number of historians. Those interested in a first-hand, unbiased but very well informed view should read Collins' autobiography.

By that time Layton had already embarked on the merchant ship *Dominion Monarch* to return to the UK. It fell to Collins to go on board the merchant ship and inform Layton of Phillips' loss. Layton returned to the War Room to resume the command of a small force largely of older ships against the attack of the well-trained and fully professional Imperial Japanese Navy.

At that time, Collins himself concluded that Singapore could not be saved.[12] In the midst of his duties, he arranged for his wife and daughter to leave by sea for Java and eventually by air for Australia.

Layton himself left for Batavia and Ceylon. He appointed Collins in command of China Force, the British and Australian ships operating with the Allies in the Dutch East Indies. Collins' new appointment merited a flag officer, instead of a middle seniority captain with the appointment (not rank) of commodore (2nd class). The command of naval vessels in local defence of the Malayan peninsula was under a separate flag officer on a level with Collins. Collins' appointment says much for Layton's confidence in him.

Ashore in Java, Collins was responsible for a force of cruisers, destroyers, corvettes and auxiliaries, the safety of British and Empire merchant ships and their port arrangements. At various stages, China Force included HMA Ships *Perth*, *Hobart*, *Yarra*, *Vendetta*, a number of *Bathurst* class ships, the depot ship *Anking*, the cruiser HMS *Exeter*, British 'D' class destroyers, the submarine HMS *Trusty*, and the Royal Indian Navy sloops *Jumna* and *Sutlej*. Collins either issued orders directly to units or assigned them to the Eastern or Western Task Forces. In the latter case, the units then reported to the Task Force Commander (as in the case of *Perth* to Admiral Doorman).

Within the Australian–British–Dutch–American (ABDA) command, China Force was more than a tactical command. ABDA was a complex top-heavy international command structure cobbled together on the other side of the world. To exacerbate Collins' problems, he had to work with a Dutch civilian administration whose home country was under Nazi rule and who (with their own families) now faced Japanese invasion. Collins held a major and extremely demanding command requiring both professional naval skills and the diplomatic ability to work amicably and effectively with at least four nationalities.

In those times an Army or Air Force officer would have been promoted to acting general or air rank. The naval practice prevented Collins receiving acting flag rank. Under the regulations, as a commodore (2nd class), Collins in theory did not have authority over Captain Howden of *Hobart* (who was senior to Collins on the post captains' list). In fairness to Howden, this does not seem to have caused any difficulty. Nevertheless, this appointment as commodore (2nd class) may be a contributory factor to Collins' not receiving appropriate recognition from some later historians.[13]

Collins' war diary for the short period of his command (only two months) shows that initially he organised independent sailings, convoys and escorts to and from Singapore. As the fall of that fortress became imminent, and Collins could see that Australian troop reinforcements would be lost, Collins put on his cap and went to the ABDA CinC (General Sir Archibald Wavell) and proposed to divert convoy BM.12. Wavell ordered that the convoy go through to Singapore, telling Collins that 'unless it does, I shall have to publish to the world that the Navy lost Singapore'.[14]

As Singapore fell, Collins' command became involved in receiving a large number of diverse merchant vessels and small naval craft filled with evacuees. The ships had to be received at Tanjong Priok, their passengers disembarked, fuel provided and sailed again. In cases where they were unfit for sea, they had to be destroyed. All this had to be done under frequent air attack, in an increasingly congested port, with the Dutch civilian authority deteriorating and with the military situation failing rapidly. The ABDA command was dissolved.

Collins' work changed to arranging destruction of shore facilities of military value, evacuations, the rescue of escapees from Singapore and islands that had fallen to the Japanese and survivors of ships sunk. The China Force War Diary is a depressing recitation of facts amounting to a steady deterioration. The ROPs of some of the *Bathurst* class illustrate the invaluable work done, often at very considerable risk, by the ships of Collins' force. These ROPs are worth a separate chapter in themselves.

Collins issued the orders to *Perth* and USS *Houston* to sail to the action in which they were sunk on 28 February. Having said that, given the geographical and military situation at the time, it is difficult to see that he could have done anything else.

When it became clear that his headquarters in Batavia would fall, Collins withdrew to Tjilatjap, on the south coast of Java, and then in the corvette HMAS *Burnie* to Fremantle. On arrival in Fremantle, Collins was extremely tense and utterly worn out.[15] There is no doubt that it fell to Collins to make some extremely hard decisions during his time in command of China Force and immediately after his return.

One of these decisions involved his former classmate Lieutenant-Commander Paul Hirst, who had left the service in the 1930s. Hirst returned to fight in 1939 and, in 1942, was in command of HMAS *Toowoomba* in China Force under Collins. After *Toowoomba* returned to Fremantle, Collins ordered Hirst to take his ship and others back to sea (now as Acting Commander and senior officer of a flotilla). Although the details are incomplete and in part contradictory, it seems that Hirst considered his ship unfit for sea and refused to sail until *Toowoomba* had been repaired. Hirst was relieved of his command, his acting rank was cancelled, and he left the service a few weeks later.[16]

On orders from Navy Office, Collins assumed the position of Commodore-in-Charge and Senior Naval Officer Western Australia (SNOWA), where his family rejoined him. They remained there until Collins' second tenure as SNOWA when he was recovering from his wounds received at Leyte.

After some months in WA, he was offered the choice of a senior British Eastern Fleet staff appointment, continuing as commodore (2nd class), or command as post captain of the cruiser HMAS *Shropshire*. Without hesitation, Collins chose the latter. Collins set off across the Pacific by air to the United States and

On 25 June 1943 Admiral Sir George H. D'Oyly Lyon, KCB, handed over the county class cruiser Shropshire *to the RAN to replace* Canberra. *This photograph shows Captain Collins, commanding officer of* Shropshire, *calling for three cheers for His Majesty the King who went aboard the ship during his Home Fleet visit. (AWM P444/214/094)*

thence by sea to Britain to commission *Shropshire* into the RAN as a replacement for HMAS *Canberra*, sunk at Savo Island.

Although no wartime cruiser sea command was undemanding, Collins' time in *Shropshire* was without the conflicting pressures and intense stress of China Force. After commissioning at Chatham and working up under Admiral Sir Bruce Fraser at Scapa Flow, Collins brought *Shropshire* home to Australia. Here she joined the Australian Squadron under Rear-Admiral Crutchley and the US Seventh Fleet's Task Force 74. There followed a period of operations characterised by preparing for supporting landing forces, escorting the forces to their assault area and then providing gunfire support.

Rear-Admiral Guy Griffiths, then a 20-year-old sub-lieutenant serving in *Shropshire*, remembers Collins as setting, by example, a high standard in uniform dress. On the bridge he was demanding but understanding, ready with a word of praise when appropriate. He delegated as normal to his officer of the watch, but was always available on call. He was a man of high principles, conducted himself with dignity and was conservative in his outlook. He came with an aura of success from *Sydney*. All the officers and sailors respected him. Ashore, he seized every opportunity to play tennis, although there were not many courts north of the Jomard Passage. In harbour, he used to take away the captain's motor boat fishing and even endeavoured (unsuccessfully) to get it to tow a surfboard fashioned by the 'chippies'.[17]

It was during this period that Collins came to appreciate the through-life support advantages of commonality of equipment with the USN. Owing to a shortage of British 8-inch bombardment ammunition, Collins' gunnery personnel devised a method of using ammunition from US sources.

In May 1944, Collins was relieved of command of *Shropshire*. In June he hoisted his broad pendant in HMAS *Australia* as commodore (1st class) in command of HMA Squadron (CCAS). Although there was no question of Collins' ability to handle the job, it was argued that he was too junior to be promoted to the rank of rear-admiral. Prime Minister Curtin's keenness to have an Australian in the job, prior to an Australian as CNS and First Naval Member of the ACNB, led to Collins' appointment. If Curtin's staff had done their research properly and watched developments in the RN Flag List, they would have found a valid precedent in the promotion in 1945 of Rear-Admiral G.N. Oliver and been free to promote Collins to flag rank in July 1945.

In his new position, Collins had administrative command of all RAN ships attached to the Seventh Fleet with tactical command of RAN ships in company and usually of a number of USN ships as well. The RAN cruisers and destroyers were generally in company. Other RAN ships, for example the landing ships, were assigned to appropriate Seventh Fleet functional units.[18]

As the senior RAN officer it fell to Collins to do his best to ensure that the RAN participated appropriately in Seventh Fleet operations leading up to the defeat of Japan. This was not always easy, with the USN trying (not always successfully) to assign a CTU instead of CTG level role to CCAS. Collins found the job demanding and stressful. He was reluctant to leave the bridge when at sea and, by the time of the Leyte operation, the strain had begun to show.[19]

His force covered PT boat operations in the Aitape and Wewak area, bombarded in the Sansapor area and took part in support operations at Morotai and elsewhere. In the invasion of the Philippines at Leyte, Collins' force was assigned to Admiral Berkey's close covering group, TG 77.3.

Collins' flagship *Australia* was hit on the bridge by a Japanese suicide plane on 21 October 1944. The casualties were heavy, with Collins himself being knocked unconscious and badly wounded. He was evacuated to Australia. It was not until the following April that he was fit enough to resume his old position of SNOWA. In July, he rehoisted his broad pendant as CCAS, this time in *Shropshire*. However, further hostile operations by the RAN Squadron were overtaken by the Japanese surrender. Collins led his Squadron to Japan and was the RAN delegate on board USS *Missouri* to watch the signing of the Japanese surrender.

Collins remained in command of the Australian Squadron until November 1946. Thus he was responsible for directing RAN ships' participation in the

*Commodore John Collins,
when commanding the
Australian Squadron.(RAN)*

repatriation of prisoners of war and troops and for patrolling the former war areas. The period saw the post-war demobilisation and substantial run-down in naval strength to peacetime levels.

After a year as a student at the Imperial Defence College in London, Collins became First Naval Member and CNS in February 1948. He was the first graduate of the RANC to become head of his profession. He considered himself too young at 49 as he saw, correctly, that it would result in his retirement well before the statutory age of 60. He was given an undertaking that this would be compensated for, as indeed it was, with his appointment as Australian High Commissioner to New Zealand after he retired from the RAN in 1955.

About halfway through his time as CNS, Collins tried very hard to get an exchange appointment as CinC of the British East Indies Squadron based in what was then known as Ceylon. The Menzies Government refused absolutely to have a British officer as CNS. Without that, the RN would not countenance the idea.

Even with forty years' hindsight, it is difficult to assess the achievements of a CNS in peacetime. Popularity among contemporaries is an unreliable measure as, in some cases, opinions can be influenced by personal disappointment and in others they mellow with the passage of time. The achievements of a peacetime CNS have to be considered in the light of prevailing political and diplomatic circumstances. During Collins' time as CNS the RAN Fleet Air Arm was successfully established (in the face of some considerable government reluctance bordering on opposition). Four *Daring* class destroyers and four *River* class frigates were ordered. The RAN participated very effectively in the Korean War and in the Malayan Emergency.

At least during his time as CNS, Collins could be a stickler for the correct observation of ceremonial duties and occasions and regarded punctuality as both important and a matter of courtesy. He and Lady Collins were active participants in official Melbourne social activity, of which there was a good deal when Navy Office was still headquartered in Melbourne.

There is no doubt that Collins had very considerable skills of persuasion and could, on occasion, be very subtle, if not Machiavellian, in the politico-defence arena. Unlike many RAN officers of his time, he also had a very considerable ability to talk to the press and radio. The ability ran in the family. John's brother Dale was a journalist and another brother, Reg, had connections in publishing.

Collins saw that it was in the interests of the RAN to talk, but some of his contemporaries, who distrusted the media, felt that Collins was inclined to 'push his own barrow' publicly. It should be acknowledged that not only Collins but also the RAN benefited from an ability which, today, is recognised as an attribute in selecting officers for the most senior posts.

Some time after Collins' return from New Zealand, Prime Minister Menzies offered him the Governor-Generalship.[20] For reasons that are not clear, Collins declined. This was Australia's loss, as Collins was well known and respected throughout Australia. The combination of his service and diplomatic experience would have served him well in Australia's prime vice-regal post.

In summary, Collins had a balance of qualities that enabled him to be outstandingly successful both ashore and afloat. It was that balance that enabled him to rise above his contemporaries and be appointed a Knight Commander of the Most Excellent Order of the British Empire, Companion of the Most Honourable Order of the Bath, Legion of Merit (USA) and the Dutch Order of Oranje Nassau.

13
The intrigue master: Commander R.B.M. Long of Naval Intelligence

Barbara Winter

It is arguable that Sir Frederick Shedden was more important than General Blamey in World War II. Other officers might have done Blamey's job as well, or better, but nobody could have replaced Shedden. Similarly, it mattered little whether the CNS was Sir Ragnar Colvin, Sir Guy Royle, or someone else, but it mattered a great deal that Commander Rupert Basil Michel Long was Director of Naval Intelligence (DNI), for that job needed a special combination of ability, personality, training and experience.

Early in 1934, Long became District Intelligence Officer, Sydney, and soon after this he was virtual DNI, although not appointed Assistant DNI until April 1936, nor DNI until August 1939. His best-known role was in developing the coastwatcher network. An extensive network already existed in 1934, but it was Long who persuaded the Naval Board and the Treasury to supply finance for extra staff and teleradios to strengthen the network in Papua New Guinea and the Solomon Islands. Long then saw a large part of the network destroyed in 1942 by the intransigence of the Army.

Besides the coastwatchers' valuable obvious work, they played an unforeseen and unrecognised role. When the Japanese learnt of their existence, they sometimes blamed the coastwatchers when their plans were unaccountably thwarted, instead of suspecting the extent of Allied wireless traffic analysis and cryptanalysis; thus they failed to change wireless procedures in ways that would have made Allied wireless intelligence in the Pacific more difficult.

The DNI was responsible for codes and ciphers, intercepts and cryptanalysis, except for the technical side of wireless procedure, which was under Commander Jack Newman, Director of Naval Communications. Thus it was Long who received the occasional Ultra decrypts of German naval Enigma signals—occasional, because the German Navy was not very active on the Australia Station until 1944, except for a few auxiliary cruisers, and their short-signal code book was never broken, nor, apparently, their cipher.

Commander Rupert Long, RAN.
(AWM 107006)

It was Long who liaised with cryptanalysts of the RN's Far East Combined Bureau in Singapore and *Kamer 14* in Batavia. It was Long who provided the ammunition for the CNS to fight Menzies for approval to set up a RAN cryptanalysis unit, the Special Intelligence Bureau, under Captain Eric Nave.

This unit was responsible for breaking merchant shipping codes, the wireless codes used in the Japanese Mandated Islands, and Japanese consular codes in Australia. The Japanese Consulate-General in Australia had no transmitter and no Morse operator. Its cables went by the Eastern Extension Australasia and China Telegraph Company. When the Consul-General wanted to receive Morse news from Japan, he had to hire a former RAN wireless officer to take it down. How did the Navy's unit get this cable traffic? Perhaps the means by which they must have been obtained is the reason why the Department of Defence has been unwilling to admit this unit's activities, even after the scope of American and British cryptanalysis became known.

But the DNI directed more than pure naval intelligence. He was the main link with overseas intelligence organisations. He had a close relationship with the DNI Admiralty and the right to report directly to him, bypassing the CNS, the ACNB and the Minister for the Navy. Long worked closely with both Admiral John Godfrey and Admiral Rushbrooke. When an Operational Intelligence Centre was set up in Britain, Long founded a Combined Operational Intelligence Centre (COIC) in Australia, and became its first director. For the first year, the burden fell almost exclusively on the Navy; the Air Force did little and the Army even less. In the early years of the war, neither the Army nor the Air Force had a full-time Director of Intelligence, and they were slow in appointing full-time staff to COIC. Only after the Pacific War began could Long hand over this role to Wing-Commander Malley. MacArthur took over COIC in 1942, but its Director was always an Australian. Under its final Director, Commander Luke, who had been trained in intelligence work by Long, COIC went right to the Philippines with MacArthur.

Long was also the Australian link with Special Operation Executive in Britain and its offshoot, the Oriental Mission in Malaya. When the Mission needed personnel, Long provided his own men. Long was the back-up for the unfortunate Lieutenant-Colonel Mawhood. He knew the scope of Mawhood's political mission on behalf of MI–6, for which his Military Mission was partly a cover. Generals Sturdee and Northcott apparently were not entitled to know, and this was largely the basis of the friction that occurred.

Long was also involved in the security aspects of Mawhood's task. Internal security, except where it concerned shipping and wharves, was not strictly naval business, but Long covered some angles of security, particularly while W.M. Hughes combined the functions of Minister for the Navy and Attorney-General. Long had a very good working relationship with Hughes, no doubt helped by the fact that Long's father-in-law, Sir Walter Carpenter, made generous donations to Hughes' electoral expenses.

Long left telephone and mail interception to Military Police Intelligence and the Commonwealth Investigation Branch, but the Navy took over wireless monitoring, and did some burglary and bribery unofficially. Long was closely involved with setting up the Commonwealth Security Service (CSS), but was never satisfied with the way it was handled. He battled with Colonel Longfield Lloyd, had little to do with Commissioner McKay, and tried to get Brigadier Simpson sacked; but Simpson, as an old school friend of Dr Evatt, could not be sacked. So Long put a very good naval liaison officer into the CSS in Canberra. A report to Churchill in 1944 by Captain Alan Hillgarth, head of RN Intelligence in the Far East, said that this man, not Simpson, was the brains of the Security Service.

Again, although internal security was not naval business, Long had agents on wharves, in Japanese social circles and in communist cells; some appear to have been former naval men who would have refused to work for the Police or Army.

When Special Operations officers from Singapore and India came to Australia in 1942, Long was their contact; he had already met most of them at a secret intelligence conference in Singapore in November 1941. Major G. Egerton Mott sought his help to set up Special Operations. Mott had no facilities, no money, no equipment and hardly any personnel. Long helped him obtain them, making Special Operations Australia and 'Z Force' possible. Captain Roy Kendall, who ran MI–6 operations in the East Indies during the war as Secret Intelligence Australia, also relied at first on Long for assistance.

Long helped Commander John Proud to found the Far Eastern Liaison Office (FELO). Working part time as a reservist, Proud had been trained in Navy Office before Long had him sent to Singapore on liaison work in connection with psychological warfare. This was a function of the Department of External Affairs, so it was Dr Evatt who had to be fought before FELO could function. Long could generally handle Evatt, and the fact that Prime Minister John Curtin had known Long's father many years previously possibly helped to bring FELO into existence. Blamey signed the authority to set up FELO, but the work was done by Long and Proud.

Long also already knew some of the Dutch Intelligence officers who formed the Netherlands Forces Intelligence Service in Australia. He knew few of the American personnel before they arrived, but he was on good terms with the Military Attache, Colonel Merle-Smith, who joined MacArthur's staff in 1942. It took some time to gain their trust. Although they appreciated his ability and took whatever intelligence he could offer, MacArthur's GHQ gave so little back that Long had to obtain US intelligence through New Zealand, where the American naval commanders were more cooperative. Long also placed agents in American units to report back to him on what he needed to know. Some of the methods these agents used to obtain this information were not quite 'Marquis of Queensberry'.

With so many secret organisations operating in Australia, there was wasteful overlapping of projects and a likelihood that they could endanger one another in the field. Long called a conference at which the Allied Intelligence Bureau was formed to coordinate irregular operations. Generals Willoughby and Sutherland signed the orders and got the credit, but again it was Long who had the idea and did the initial work.

A surprising fact is the extent to which Long engaged in foreign espionage. Australian overseas intelligence-gathering did not begin post-war with the Australian Secret Intelligence Service (ASIS). It did not even begin with Long, but he extended and refined it. It was said that he ran more than 150 agents personally, and he did it on a minuscule budget. Captains of Australian vessels on Asian and Pacific routes reported to him and brought him 'safe-hand' mail. Pilots of Qantas flying boats reported to him or to District Intelligence Officers.

When information was needed from Portuguese Timor, Long sent up David Ross, a graduate of the RANC, as a Qantas agent, and Paymaster Lieutenant John Whittaker, undercover as a civilian clerk. Long also arranged for filmmaker Freddie Daniell to send a cameraman to Dili to film everything he could on the pretext of making a newsreel on Timor. To get from New Caledonia information not readily obtainable by official British and Australian representatives, he acquired the services of Major Oughton, representative of a nickel-mining company, and Long was very much involved in preventing the Vichy French in Noumea from handing the island and its nickel over to the Japanese. It will never

Lungga, Guadalcanal, Solomon Islands, 14 October 1943. Lieutenant Commander I. Pryce-Jones (standing sixth from left), the Deputy Supervising Intelligence Officer, Naval Intelligence Division, RAN, with his staff and visiting coastwatchers at his headquarters camp. On the left is Lieutenant A.R. Evans, DSC, RANVR, who rescued Lieutenant John F. Kennedy, USN, later President Kennedy, when his PT boat was sunk. The dog is 'Coco' who always gave warning of approaching Japanese aircraft before the air-raid sirens sounded. Lungga was the collection and relay point for operational intelligence gathered by the coastwatcher network. (AWM P1672.002)

be possible to trace most of those who worked covertly for the Naval Intelligence Division.

After mid-1942, Long did not have to control his work virtually alone. A Special Division of FELO under Lieutenant-Commander Paul McGuire handled dirty tricks, such as forging Japanese documents and currency. FELO also sent out intelligence-gathering parties, sometimes duplicating the work of Special Operations, and sometimes succeeding where other parties failed. When McGuire was sent to Britain in 1945, FELO Special Operations was taken over by Major Alfred Brookes, who later became head of ASIS, in a direct line back through McGuire and Proud to Long.

To sum up the value of Long's work: Of his coastwatcher network, Admiral Halsey said that the Coastwatchers saved Guadalcanal, and Guadalcanal saved the Pacific. MacArthur said they shortened the Pacific war by six months. In his report to Churchill, Captain Hillgarth said that Long had helped found every intelligence body in Australia, and in 1944 was still influencing them for the good of everybody. Several people who worked closely with Long have said that, through Hillgarth, and through the DNI Admiralty, Long was one of the few Australians who could get Australian views and assessments through Churchill.

Echoes of his influence still reverberate today. Long helped found the organisations that preceded the Defence Signals Directorate, ASIO and ASIS. He trained many of the men who staffed them, but when he was offered the job of head of ASIO, he turned it down, saying that he had not devoted his life to intelligence in order to spy on his fellow Australians.

After Long died in January 1960, Hillgarth wrote that he had never met anyone who combined such a talent for intrigue with downright honesty. Heading an intelligence organisation is a very difficult and demanding task, as problems with ASIO and ASIS—and especially with the CIA—have shown. Combining the intelligence arms of the three services into a Joint Intelligence Bureau should in theory make for efficiency and diminish service rivalry. However, if someone is appointed to the job because it is the turn of that branch of the services, and not because he is the best person available, the arrangement would not be for the best. Not all appointees would necessarily be a Long.

14
The RAN Hydrographic Branch, 1942–45

John G. Betty

The Hydrographic Branch of the RAN, now known as the Hydrographic Service, celebrated its 75th anniversary in October 1995.[1] In 1943 it was undergoing major expansion and there was a shortage of hydrographers. Some Permanent Service officers had pre-war experience in hydrography but the majority were reservists who seemed to have been absorbed into the Hydrographic Branch by being serving officers on ships taken over by the Branch. It would appear that there were only two Reserve officers with surveying experience and no one else, not even the Permanent Service officers, had any formal surveying qualifications—everyone had been trained on-the-job.

When three young engineers, of whom I was one, trained in surveying techniques, offered their services, the Branch apparently saw it as an opportunity to acquire some badly needed expertise. If deck officers could be trained on-the-job to be hydrographers, surely engineer/surveyors could be trained on-the-job as deck officers. After a very brief and hastily organised course at HMAS *Penguin* we soon found ourselves keeping watch on survey ships in New Guinea. We must surely have been the only deck officers who had virtually no naval training whatsoever.

My service in the Navy covered a very significant period in the story of the Hydrographic Branch. It was the reputation and experience earned by the Branch in those years that led to the development of the Hydrographic Service of today with its properly trained personnel working in custom-built survey ships. Initially I had little idea of what the work involved but soon realised that it complemented my desire to build things. Not only were we doing our part in the war effort, but the work had a constructive component. Every day we spent on the survey grounds, the work contributed in a very small way to making the sea lanes just that little bit safer for the seafarer. The work was sometimes hazardous, often arduous but never boring. But first, a brief account of the pre-war Branch to

152

HMAS Moresby, *as modified for survey operations in 1944.* Moresby *was transferred from the RN in 1925 and during the war served as a convoy escort and anti-submarine training vessel before reverting to her original survey role. She was paid off in 1946 and broken up the following year. (J. Betty)*

form a background to my account, which is based primarily on my service in HMA Ships *Moresby* and *Warrego*.

Pre-war operations

Although the RAN was established some ten years after Federation, it was not until 1920, when the Admiralty presented the sloop HMAS *Geranium* as a survey ship to work with HMS *Fantome* in Northern Australia, that the RAN assumed responsibility for hydrographic surveying in Australian waters. In 1925, the RAN acquired HMS *Silvio*, renamed her *Moresby*, and *Fantome* was paid off. *Moresby* was one of four '24 Class' Fleet sweeping sloops built for the RN in 1918 and converted to serve as survey ships in 1923, the conversion requiring major reconstruction. It was not until 1964 that the Hydrographic Service acquired a survey ship designed and built specifically for hydrographic work—the second HMAS *Moresby*.

In 1927 *Geranium* was paid off and *Moresby* continued the work alone and intermittently until the outbreak of war in September 1939. *Moresby* then returned to general service, initially as an anti-submarine warfare instruction unit and later as a convoy escort vessel. In 1940, *Moresby* briefly reverted to her survey role when she was engaged in the survey of the Great North East Channel in Torres Strait under Commander Martin. Without her, the Hydrographic Branch had no survey ship and work was largely restricted to the use of Survey Motor Boats (SMBs).

The New Guinea surveys

In June 1942, General MacArthur authorised the construction of airstrips at Milne Bay to counter the growing Japanese threat to New Guinea. The NOIC at Port Moresby, Commander R.B. Hunt (a senior officer in the Hydrographic Branch) arranged for a survey of the Gili Gili anchorage in Milne Bay to be undertaken in July 1942 by Lieutenant-Commander George Tancred in HMAS *Kwato*, a 60-ft island trader recently commissioned as a survey tender. This survey assisted a rapid build-up of the defences of Milne Bay leading to the repulse in August of the attempted Japanese landing. It was the first step in the Hydrographic Branch's expanding role in the South-West Pacific campaign.

Following the defeat of the Japanese in the Owen Stanley Ranges in November 1942, the Allies commenced their operation to recapture Buna and Gona. Due to the difficulty of supplying the investing forces by air or along the Kokoda Track, a tenuous supply line was established along the coast from Milne Bay using local small craft. The threat of attack by Japanese aircraft, ships and submarines based in New Britain forced these vessels to find their way along an uncharted and dangerous inner coastal route rather than using a navigationally safer deep-water route north of the Trobriand Islands.

The Hydrographic Branch was given a challenge—the task of surveying and establishing an inshore route from Milne Bay to Cape Nelson, east of Buna and well within reach of the Japanese. In October 1942, the sloop *Warrego*, under Lieutenant-Commander Tancred's direction, commenced a one week's survey from East Cape to Cape Nelson through Goschen and Ward Hunt Straits establishing a safe route from Milne Bay to the southern side of Cape Nelson. The waters around Cape Nelson and along the coast to Cape Ward Hunt, about 100 nautical miles north-west of Cape Nelson, had uncharted reefs extending up to 50 nautical miles offshore. In November 1942, Tancred in HMAS *Stella* (previously the CSIR fisheries research trawler *Wareen*) and Lieutenant Cody in HMAS *Polaris* (a small local vessel taken over by the Navy) under the direction of Commander Karl Oom, commenced a survey to establish a safe inshore route around Cape Nelson. They erected two lighted beacons onshore near Tufi Harbour to indicate the channel by which to approach the Cape—these beacons became famous as the 'Tufi Leads'. The safe channel then skirted Cape Nelson between one and two miles from the shore to a point near Porlock Harbour at the eastern end of Dyke Ackland Bay.

As a matter of expediency, their task was to find a passage through the reefs rather than to chart every obstruction in the area. This was the reverse of the usual survey procedure when a safe route was determined after locating all obstructions to navigation in the particular area. Surveys were also made of harbours between Cape Nelson and Buna to enable the small supply ships to discharge troops and supplies for the Buna assault.

In January 1943, HMAS *Whyalla* became the first actual warship to join the survey team and hydrographers quickly established a route from Milne Bay to

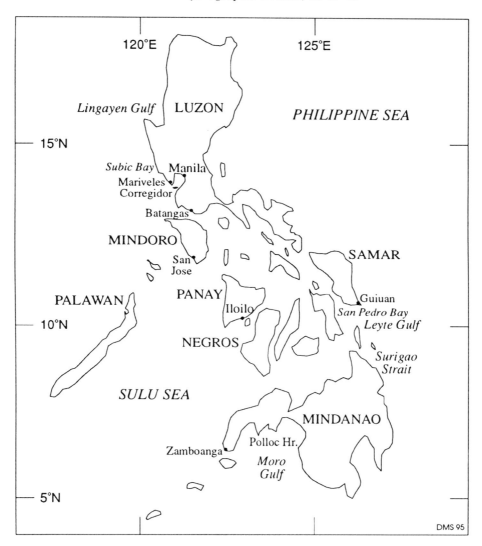

Map 14.2: *The Philippines*

Torres Strait

Following the end of the New Guinea campaign, TU 70.5.2, comprising four Australian survey ships (*Shepparton*, *Polaris*, *Winter* and *ML 820*), commenced work in Torres Strait. They were joined in this work by the RN survey ship HMS *Challenger* and were assisted by four Australian minesweepers (HMAS

Durraween, Goolgwai, Samuel Benbow and *Echuca*) in sweeping for coral outcrops.

Torres Strait is a notoriously dangerous stretch of water and careful sounding was required to ensure a safe route for capital ships. The TU's prime task was to examine the western approaches to the Strait and to sound a channel varying from 20 to 30 miles wide from Cape van Diemen, forming the north-western tip of Melville Island, to Booby Island west of Thursday Island—a distance of some 600 naut. miles. Although the Great North-Eastern Channel through the Barrier Reef had been surveyed by Commander Martin in *Moresby* in December 1940, it was swept as a check by the four minesweeper consorts.

The Timor Sea survey

In July 1944, TU 70.5.3, under the direction of Commander Little in *Moresby*, commenced work on the survey of a channel approximately 60 nautical miles wide through the Timor Sea from Scott Reef to Darwin. The work included a detailed survey of Scott Reef and harbour surveys at Darwin, Port Nelson and Snake Bay in Melville Island. Four Australian survey ships were involved (*Moresby, Shepparton, Stella* and *Sleuth*) assisted by a further four AMS (HMA Ships *Castlemaine, Echuca, Horsham* and *Junee*) as consorts for the sounding of the 650 nautical mile long channel.

By the end of July 1945, TU 70.5.1 had basically completed its task in the Philippines and the remaining work was handed over to local USN authorities. In Borneo, *Lachlan* was tidying up after the landings; TU 70.5.2 had virtually completed its work in Torres Strait where *Shepparton* had replaced *Challenger*; and TU 70.5.3 was still working in the northern approaches to Darwin linking up the work of the Timor Sea and the Torres Strait surveys. The dropping of the atom bombs abruptly changed the situation and the war formally ended on 15 August 1945. Survey work was immediately curtailed and the ships were re-allocated for re-occupation duties.

A day in the life . . .

A survey ship usually anchored at night when it was on the survey grounds. The day usually began at 0600 with 'All Hands' followed by breakfast at 0630. The boats were then prepared for the day's operations to be ready to leave the ship at 0730; they were not expected to return before 1730. Shore parties, tasked to set up marks, clear lines of sight, carry out theodolite observations and the like, often required extra hands to carry all the equipment necessary. There was no shortage of volunteers and they included sailors from all Divisions as a 'run ashore' was highly sought after.

As soon as the preliminary onshore work was sufficiently advanced, the sounding would commence. Sometimes the area where the SMBs were to operate

Erecting a sounding mark, during the survey of Madang Harbour, May 1944. Moresby *is at anchor in the background. (J. Betty)*

required an hour or more's travel from the ship and they would spend the rest of the day in sounding.

Shore parties were usually unarmed—an exception being during the first few days of the Madang survey where the Japanese had just been evicted from the town and a few 'stragglers' were reported in the vicinity. Shore parties were usually so heavily loaded with equipment that firearms would have been just an added burden. The SMBs would only be armed when working close inshore to enemy-held coastline.

While the boat parties were away, the ship often weighed anchor and worked offshore, sounding in deeper water, laying or recovering beacons or running the taut wire. The ship usually returned to anchor before 1730 for the return of the boats. The boats were unloaded, cleaned and refuelled for the next day's operations and the crews were then free for dinner and to enjoy their last dog watch. After a shower and a change, the survey officers assembled in the wardroom for dinner at 1900. Each evening the CO's Night Orders book setting out the work to be done the next day and allocating tasks was delivered to the wardroom. Every officer, including non-surveying personnel such as the medical officer, the paymaster and the engineer, was to read and initial the order book.

After dinner, the hydrographers adjourned to the survey chart room to enter up their day's work, compute any calculations, plot results and transfer soundings corrected for tide from the echo sounder charts to the plotting boards. The recorders and boat cox'ns were shown the night orders and details of personnel and equipment required for the next day were determined. Normally, the hydrographers would retire to their bunks by 2300 to be ready for the next day's work at 0630.

The surveying operation

The prime aim of the survey was to produce a sufficiently accurate chart with enough detail to enable the navigation of vessels safely through the particular area. A nautical chart is essentially a topographic map with certain unique characteristics:

- To the seafarer, details of the seabed are of prime importance. For the most part, the seabed is invisible to both the hydrographer and to the navigator and has to be defined by spot levels (soundings) and contour lines.
- The accuracy of the chart is determined by the method used in locating these soundings. Both the hydrographer and the navigator using the chart are constrained by having to rely on hand-held instruments working from a floating and unstable platform.

The techniques used in hydrographic surveying had, with the exception of the introduction of the echo sounder after World War I, remained virtually unchanged since the beginning of the nineteenth century. Surveying methods were still based on optical observations using theodolites for onshore work and sextants for offshore work. Even with the introduction of satellite navigation and other electronic equipment, the basic principles remain the same and the modern hydrographer faces the same difficulties and challenges—only some of the tools are different

The first task was to establish a grid or network of reference points. Where the area to be surveyed was coastal or within an archipelago, most of these reference points would be onshore and their location determined with sufficient accuracy by standard geodetic techniques using a theodolite. Where the survey grounds were out of sight of land, other methods were adopted. Usually a grid of floating beacons was set out, their locations being determined by sextant observations supported by taut-wire measurements where a fine piano wire fed from a drum containing 140 miles of wire was paid out over the stern of the survey ship, the length run out being read from a dynamometer. At the end of the run, the wire was cut and left on the seabed.

For a land-based grid, a baseline was set out and measured on a level, unobstructed area such as a suitable beach. The location and orientation of the baseline was determined by sun or star observations at one or both ends of the baseline using a theodolite. Triangulation stations were then established so that the lines of sight joining the stations formed a series of triangles covering the whole area. The stations were usually set up on prominent hills or promontories or on offshore islets and the angles between adjoining stations were measured. When observing at each station, bearings were observed to all significant features such as hill and mountain peaks, prominent trees, buildings, offshore islands and the like. In this way, the coordinates of each triangulation station and observed feature could be calculated and plotted.

Triangulation stations were usually marked by a brass plug or plate set in concrete or drilled into a permanent rock. A guyed bamboo pole with a large red and white flag was set up directly over the mark to form a target for observations from adjoining stations (survey ships could usually be identified by the rack of bamboo poles on the upper deck). Sounding marks were also set up along the coast so that the SMBs always had at least three marks to work on when sounding. These marks were usually a small flag or, in some cases, they could be a readily distinguished rock or tree marked with white paint if necessary.

All triangulation stations and marks were given names for identification. These were generally short (4–6 letters) and related to some significant feature or circumstance. This sometimes led to unexpected results. While erecting a sounding mark on the shore at the northern point forming the entrance to Alexishafen, I found an empty KB Lager bottle and identified the mark by the letters 'KB'. Some months later, in the Hydrographic Drawing Office in Cremorne, Sydney, I noticed that the point had been labelled 'Kaybe Point'.

The locations of all stations and marks were plotted on a master sheet from which they were transferred to sheets glued to plotting boards covering the particular area to be sounded for use on the SMBs. The lines of soundings to be run were drawn in pencil about 5 mm apart on the plotting boards. The actual distance between each line was, therefore, a function of the scale of the chart. If the survey was to a scale of 1:25 000, the lines of soundings were thus 125 metres apart.

The SMB was positioned at the beginning of the first line by observing simultaneously angles to three contiguous sounding marks and plotting the position with a three-arm station pointer. When the correct position was reached, the run was started along a predetermined compass bearing.

Fixes were taken at about two to three minute intervals and the course was corrected as required so that a straight line was run. The boats usually sounded at about 6 knots so that in a 1:25 000 survey the 'fixes' were about 550 metres apart (about 20–25 mm apart on the plot). On a 'good' day, 150 fixes could be achieved representing about 50 nautical miles of sounding.

The survey motor boats

The SMBs were the hydrographers' 'workhorses'. Without these sturdy and versatile boats, the larger survey ships would not be able to operate. They were essential for carrying the hydrographers ashore to set up and observe at survey stations and marks, to set out and measure baselines, delineate coastlines and, most importantly, to enable soundings to be taken close inshore where the survey ship could not operate. In accordance with an RN tradition dating back to the early nineteenth century, SMBs were all officially named—the only non-commissioned craft in the Navy to be so honoured.

The Hydrographic Branch had nine SMBs working during World War II. The four oldest SMBs were the 25-ft *Alert* and the 28-ft *Endeavour*, *Fantome* and *Hearty*. These four boats were fitted with Kitchen rudders which made them extremely manoeuvrable. There were five more modern 34-ft SMBs—*Sandfly*, *Sealark*, *Dart*, *Seamew* and *Mermaid*. *Hearty* foundered near Wewak on 10 June 1944 while being towed from Madang to Hollandia by YMS *73*; in August 1944 *Sealark* suffered a similar fate while being escorted by *Benalla*. Only the larger survey ships (*Moresby*, *Warrego*, *Lachlan*) were equipped with davits capable of hoisting SMBs, otherwise the SMBs had to proceed between survey grounds under their own power or be towed. Following the loss of *Hearty* and *Sealark*, the SMBs had to be hoisted aboard larger ships when moving between survey grounds.

There were several 25-ft fast motor launches carried by the larger survey ships which, although not SMBs, were unofficially given names such as *Blowfly*, *Dolphin* and *Flying Fish*.

The end of hostilities

When hostilities ceased, the Hydrographic Branch had 56 officers (15 permanent service, 41 reservists) classified as surveyors. All the reservists and four of the junior Permanent Service officers were graded as assistant surveyors fourth class for which they were paid an additional 2/6 (25 cents) per day specialist pay. This grade and rate of pay was established by the RN in 1854—90 years later it was still unchanged. The other, more senior Permanent Service officers, with considerable pre-war hydrographic experience, were classified as charge surveyors or surveyors first class.

The hydrographers were ably supported by survey recorders—mostly petty officers or leading seamen—who had been with the Branch in earlier times or who had also been trained on-the-job. Anyone who showed an interest or aptitude for the work was readily accepted for training as a survey recorder and could become a valuable member of the team.

Branch personnel were a typical cross-section of the Service and most seemed to have entered into the work with vigour and enthusiasm. Although sometimes strafed, bombed and shelled while carrying out their duties, only a small number of men were wounded, none were killed. Their work was recognised by the award of two OBEs, thirteen DSCs, four DSMs and fourteen MIDs with two US Legion of Merits.

SMB Endeavour, *while attached to* HMAS Moresby, *during the survey of Port Nelson WA in November 1944. (J. Betty)*

Conclusion

During the Pacific War, a total of eighteen RAN ships had been engaged in survey duties on a more or less full-time basis and a further seventeen ships acted as consorts and auxiliaries. When the eleven US and one RN ships were added, a total of 47 ships had been engaged in hydrographic work in the SWPA under the direction of the Hydrographic Branch. Survey ships sometimes suffered damage due to enemy action, but apart from the sinking of the SMBs *Hearty* and *Sealark*, no survey ships were lost.

Except when defending themselves against air attack, survey ships were rarely involved in a combat role—that was not their function. Nevertheless, the personnel and ships of the Hydrographic Branch formed part of the spearhead of the Allied thrust in the South-West Pacific. There is little doubt that their work played a significant part in the success of the Allies in their prosecution of the war. Unfortunately there has been little appreciation or acknowledgment of their work and few people are fully aware of the nature and extent of their involvement. The full story of the Hydrographic Branch has yet to be written.

The work of the Hydrographic Service continues today and there are now many men and women of the Service working on the northern and western coasts of the continent. It is hoped that they are deriving the same sense of satisfaction and achievement experienced by this author.

15
Touching on Fairmiles

Marsden Hordern

Touching on Fairmiles commences by touching on Albert Noel Campbell Macklin—in the twentieth century, something of a Renaissance man—visionary, industrialist, adventurer, engineer, and father of the Fairmiles. Born in 1886, the son of a wealthy barrister, he was educated at Eton, where he is said to have kept a young lion. This interest later blossomed and led to his becoming a big game hunter, and a photographer, who produced an early film on Africa's wild animals. As a Captain in the Royal Horse Artillery during World War I, he fought in France, was wounded and invalided. He then joined the RNVR as a lieutenant and served with the Dover Patrol. After World War I Macklin took up car racing, flying, yachting, ballooning, aerial advertising and vehicle manufacturing, which he carried out behind his home at Fairmile in Surrey.

From these modest beginnings sprang the vast Fairmile operation of World War II.[1] He started this shortly before the outbreak of war, when, convinced that England would need small vessels to counter the German's E-boats, he began building craft designed for this purpose, and by 1939 he was supplying 'Fairmiles', as he called them, to the RN. The business grew rapidly. Soon he was employing 550 people, building eight different types of Fairmiles on 140 slipways located in various parts of the United Kingdom. He was also contracting out work to other manufacturers who found themselves meeting new and challenging demands: a linoleum factory turned propeller shafts, wire-makers produced rudders, a bell foundry made propellers, and a radiator firm fuel tanks. By 1941 one Fairmile was being turned out every 36 hours, and in all 703 vessels were built in England. For these achievements Macklin was deservedly knighted.

Some Fairmiles were produced in kit form for assembly overseas, and twelve of these came to Australia. Built to an Admiralty design by Sydney Graham, the 35 B-Type Fairmiles that served in the RAN were Australia's smallest class of warship and second only in number to the *Bathurst* class corvettes.

With a displacement of approximately 90 tons, their construction varied a little but they were generally 112-feet long, with a beam of 17-feet 10-inches. They drew 4 feet 1 inch forward and just over 5 feet aft. Their ground tackle included one 120 pound and one 80 pound CQR ('Ploughshare') anchor, and four shackles of 3/16 inch chain, all worked by a backbreaking hand winch. Fairmiles were powered with twin 650 hp, Hall Scott Defender petrol engines and could carry 2305 imperial gallons of fuel. At their top speed of slightly over 18 knots their range was 600 miles and at 12 knots 1500 miles.

The B-Type Fairmile was an excellent sea boat, and served in many roles— escorting convoys, hunting submarines, transporting troops, freighting ammunition, bombarding enemy positions, plucking ditched airmen from the sea, and carrying out 'cloak and dagger' operations far behind enemy lines. But they had their weaknesses. Being long and narrow, they needed sensible handling in a short, steep, head sea to prevent 'pile-driving', and care had to be taken running before a large following sea when the square stern could be caught and driven sideways down a wave, placing the ship in danger of broaching.

In 1942 I was appointed the sub-lieutenant of HMAML *814* fresh off Halvorsen Brothers slipway in Sydney, with everything brand new—gleaming paint and shining varnish. From forepeak to tiller flat floated exciting smells of Stockholm tar, marlin, linseed oil, spun yarn, sisal and Manila cordage. It was ordered to Australia's north-western front—the first Fairmile to sail north for the tropical war zone.

814 was built before any kits had arrived in Australia with double diagonal Huon Pine planking, between which was a layer of heavy canvas impregnated with linseed oil. She took nine months to build, was completed in November 1942, and cost £30 000. The armament of the RAN's Fairmiles varied enormously and *814* first faced the Japanese with a single shot Rolls Royce 2-pounder forward, two Lewis machine-guns by the bridge, a Vickers abaft the funnel, and a 20 mm Oerlikon. She was fitted with a Type 134 anti-submarine detecting set, a Y-Gun for throwing two 500-pound depth charges, and carried fourteen more charges in deck racks. Small arms for landing and boarding parties included Smith and Wesson revolvers, Thompson submachine guns, Lee-Enfield rifles, bayonets and hand grenades. Later vessels were much more heavily armed—one even carried a bazooka.

814 also had on her bridge a Schmerly rocket. This alarming Heath Robinson-style invention was designed to divert low-flying aircraft. It was supposed to be fired five seconds before the enemy arrived overhead by standing clear and pulling a lanyard. It required some courage to use. The rocket rose with a frightening whoosh, hurling sparks and smoke down onto the bridge and exploded in the air leaving a wire suspended from a parachute which, it was hoped, would wrap itself around the aircraft. It was a terrifying sound.

Fairmiles were designed for short periods at sea in the cold confined waters of the English Channel and operating from bases with accommodation facilities

HMA Motor Launch 814 at speed in 1943. She is armed with a Rolls Royce 2-pounder Mark XIV gun forward and a 20 mm Oerlikon AA gun aft. Machine-guns are mounted at the back of the bridge and on the centreline amidships. Depth charges on cradles and throwers can also be seen. 814 has been camouflaged in a scheme of three shades of grey. (AWM 301793)

ashore. They had no showers, and *814* sailed north to serve under the fierce heat of a tropical sun without awnings.

The Fairmiles' complement was generally three officers and seventeen men. They were furnished with a small spirit stove and two small kerosene-operated 'Silent Knight' refrigerators. On tropical service there was little fresh food. Powdered egg and milk and tinned 'M&V' rations were standard fare. For lifesaving there were rubber 'Mae West' inflatable vests, a 10-foot clinker-built wooden dinghy with oars, and two Carley rafts.

So much for the equipment of a Fairmile. What was it like to serve in one? Step into a time machine, turn the clock back 52 years, and board ML *814* on a 'cloak and dagger' operation. But as the average age of her ship's company was 21, some of you may have to try and imagine what it was like to be that age, at war and frequently frightened. (The adventures of those six days were recorded in my war journal at the time and are still crystal clear in my mind.)

It is now the month of July 1943 and you are one of the ship's company of ML *814*, serving with her sister ship *815* on Australia's north-western front, based on Darwin. Our hard-pressed guerrillas are still fighting overwhelming numbers of Japanese in Timor, and the RAN has suffered severe losses in trying to maintain them. At first the little fisheries protection vessels *Kuru* and *Vigilant* ran the gauntlet. On one occasion the *Kuru* was sighted by Japanese planes and subsequently attacked for seven hours. The RAN pressed the destroyer *Voyager* and several of its corvettes into this service and lost the *Voyager* and the *Armidale* with many lives. Some of the *Armidale*'s men drifted for a week on a makeshift raft and died very slowly.

It is the morning of 26 July 1943, ML *814* is lying peacefully at her buoy in Darwin harbour near her sister ship *815* and the burnt out hull of the *Neptuna* resembling a huge stranded whale. Sunshine sparkles on the water and above the town scavenging kites circle on thermals. The signal tower ashore starts flashing—'*814–814–814*'. You pick up the bridge Aldis lamp and tell it to proceed. The message reads 'Commanding Officer to report to Operations forthwith'.

A jeep collects the captain at the Commonwealth Airways' jetty. Something is afoot. The crew speculates. A ditched airman? Torpedoed ship? Air–sea rescue cover for a strike on the Tanimbar Islands? Time passes. The jeep comes down the hill, dry-season dust flying from its wheels. The captain arrives, tension on his face. He gestures the other two officers down to the wardroom, drops into his chair, flings his cap across the room, calls loudly on that member of the Holy Trinity who assumed human form 2000 years ago, and continues, 'What a job they've got for us, we're off to bloody Timor, I'll miss the nurses' dance'. Rough justice! For many months that captain has drawn the lucky straw for social nights ashore.

This operation is to succour our commandos and at the request of the neutral Portuguese Government try to rescue a large number of its nationals fleeing from the Japanese and encumbering our men. MLs *814* and *815* will both go. The Japs will be listening and strict radio silence must be observed. RAAF Beaufighters from 31 Squadron will give some air cover but only one at a time. Moral support. We will have to go over slowly at 10 knots to conserve fuel for the high-speed dash home. Two of the Beaufighter pilots who will cover us in relays come aboard to talk. They are not amused. For them this is a horrible assignment. The Japanese have air supremacy over the Timor Sea and the idea of their circling round and round two Fairmiles crawling across 300 miles of such dangerous water makes them feel like sacrificial lambs. One lets slip that his heavy twin-engined Beaufighter is no match for fast manoeuvrable Zeros, and that if they pounce he could only make one pass and go full speed for home 10 feet above the water. You commiserate and express complete confidence in the Air Force.

Preparations begin and butterflies flutter in stomachs as carpenters arrive to build a large skid over the quarterdeck. You have to crouch climbing out of the wardroom companionway—a 28-foot canvas assault boat is lashed to it. Outside

The burned and battered hulk of HMAS Voyager *ashore at Betano, Portuguese Timor.
After service in the famous 'Scrap Iron Flotilla' in the Mediterranean,* Voyager *had
returned to Australia in late 1941. On the evening of 23 September 1942* Voyager
*went aground while disembarking troops in Japanese-occupied Timor. After
unsuccessful attempts to free the ship she was wrecked by her own crew assisted by
the efforts of Japanese bombers.* Voyager's *crew were picked up without loss by HMA
Ships* Warrnambool *and* Kalgoorlie. *(AWM 043828)*

Timor's surf it will be pushed into the water. It cannot be lifted back on board
but it costs money and you have to bring it back and that will slow your escape.

An officer arrives with a fake Japanese ensign and tells you to hoist it on
the way over as a *'ruse de guerre'*. 'Sailing under false colours' sounds better
in French. You discuss this with 'Chips' Wood, the first lieutenant, and D'Arcy
Kelly, the signalman in charge of flags, and decide that if you are caught it will
be fighting under the White Ensign not the Rising Sun. They might use blunt
swords. There is no need to worry the captain with such trivialities so you shove
the fake Jap flag into a potato locker. In 1994, 51 years later, it will be presented
to the Australian War Memorial at a ceremony attended by seven surviving
members of *814*'s company who refused to sail under false colours. The flag
and its story touching on Fairmiles are now preserved for posterity in our national
capital.

Cyril Alcorn, the Port Chaplain, affectionately known as 'The Bishop', comes
aboard just before sailing time. Big and gentle, he doesn't seem to care whether
you are Catholic, Protestant or nothing. You gather round him near the two-
pounder and in a quiet prayer he commits you into God's hands as you are about

to 'pass through the waters'. Some wag makes the crack that the waters are passing through him right now. It breaks the tension and raises a laugh. But God is now officially involved and that helps. The 'Bishop' shakes each man's hand and gives him a small piece of sticky, melting, 'Comforts Fund' chocolate. Remembering the fate of the *Armidale*'s men you hoard it for raft rations. Alcorn takes the letters some have written to parents, promises to post them if necessary, but says he will hand them back to you in a week or two. A Portuguese pilot comes aboard and is given the bunk in the wheelhouse under the chart table.

814 has had some lively moments recently and now you are off again on new adventures. With *815* she slips out of Darwin Harbour at night bound for King's Cove on the north of Melville Island and next day anchors there close to the ruins of Fort Dundas built by the Redcoats in 1824. HMAS *Coolebar* is waiting. Once a coaster she is now a converted coal-fired minesweeper. Her genial, pipe-smoking captain, Lieutenant Ken Shatwell RANVR, is an older man—probably about thirty-two. One day he will become a professor, and Dean of the Faculty of Law at Sydney University. There is little about him now to suggest such dignity. *Coolebar* carries 44-gallon drums of highly inflammable 100-octane petrol which must be slung on board and pumped into the Fairmiles' tanks to replace the fuel used on the 120-mile run from Darwin. Fuelling Fairmiles from drums on deck is very dangerous and there are strict rules: no smoking, break all electrical switches and wear rubber-soled shoes, lest a spark from a nail on the armour-plated deck should become a ball of fire. But Shatwell—no Fairmile man—does not seem worried. He superintends the operation with glowing pipe in mouth, full of cheerful anecdote. And when, sensing your fears, he waves his pipe at the *Coolebar*'s funnel breathing smoke and sparks above the petrol drums, his pipe suddenly seems irrelevant. He takes the secret code books, they must not fall into Japanese hands. He also takes the depth charges. They weigh four tons and in a quartering sea Fairmiles can roll them under. If this operation succeeds there may be four tons of Portuguese on the upper deck and Fairmiles were not designed for that as well as their depth charges.

For hours the ship lies alongside *Coolebar* while the heavy drums of petrol are slung aboard by her steam winch and the depth charges are manhandled from their racks and hoisted onto her deck. At last the work is done and the Fairmiles slip their lines and anchor in the quiet cove. Night falls. It is time for sleep.

About noon the next day they begin their 300-mile crawl across the Timor Sea under a cloudless sky with unlimited visibility—perfect for Japanese reconnaissance aircraft. At night the constellation of Scorpio with its great red heart-star, Antares, arches above your circling mast. It also shines on the nurses and soldiers dancing and drinking beer in Darwin. The Captain curses his luck. Next day Timor's towering mountains loom on the western horizon. They are 10 000 feet high and something to see after the flat sameness of the Arnhem

171

Land coast. Early that afternoon you sail over the grave of the *Armidale* a thousand fathoms below your keel and you keep your fingers crossed.

Flight-Lieutenant Ray White's Beaufighter, which has been escorting you, drops lower to avoid detection from the shore. It reduces his chances if he is attacked. Each time he comes round he puts his hand out of the cockpit window with what might be a cheerful 'thumbs up' sign, or a rude gesture, and then gives a friendly wave. The long afternoon wears on as the two Fairmiles creep slowly in. Sacks are draped over wheelhouse windows to prevent the westering sun flashing signals to the Japanese. Tinned rations and extra cans of water are stowed in the dinghy and life rafts. The Beaufighter circles for his last low sweep. He passes just above the bridge and the blue and white roundels on his wings and his cannon muzzles look larger than ever before. This is the last time you will have that warm feeling that he is there. He waves, the roar of his radial engines rises and, as he banks steeply, his Aldis lamp flashes. Eight letters, but all that he can say, 'Good Luck'. He levels out, opens his throttles and disappears over the south-eastern horizon toward Darwin. Now the Fairmiles are alone.

You calculate that the Japanese patrols will also be returning and go below to try and get some sleep for whatever the night might hold. Suddenly, the strident clatter of the action stations alarm jerks you awake and the engines roar as full power is ordered on the telegraphs. The ship shudders as she builds up fighting speed and you scramble on deck to your gun. Every one is wearing a 'Mae West' and steel helmet and all binoculars are trained on an aircraft circling over the northern horizon. It makes a leisurely turn and flies towards you, turns again and flies away. He has not seen you in the gathering dusk and you wonder if he will be having powdered eggs, or saki and rice for tea.

The island is now close. You can pick out individual trees. The Portuguese pilot becomes agitated and voices rise on the bridge as he identifies the darkening coast. You are five miles too far south-west, approaching a Japanese post and turn to starboard. A faint blue light flashes the secret rendezvous letter from the shore. You give the coded reply and three fires erupt on the beach 50 yards apart. You have either found the commandos or the operation has been betrayed and it is a trap. The first boat through the surf will settle that. Anchors splash into the water in four fathoms outside the first surge, the cable is broken and the anchor secured to a stout Manila line. Beside the winch is an axe. At the first sign of trouble the ship will cut and run. If you are ashore—bad luck.

The engines stop and there is an eerie silence, save for the sound of low surf breaking on the beach. Spicy scents float out from the land and all is bustle as the big boat slides into the water and weapons, ammunition, food, medicines and tins of two-shilling pieces are hurriedly loaded. You climb down the scrambling net into the boat where four bearded sailors man the oars. They are armed with knives and revolvers and wear heavy boots in case they have to take to the mountains. They look like extras for the *Pirates of Penzance* but none is singing.

Some of the crew of ML 814 in 1943. (M. Hordern)

You stand in the stern holding the long sweep oar and give the order to shove off.

The ship looks large as you draw away. The first wave lifts the boat, carries her forward, slips under her bow and breaks ahead. The surf is low but it still needs care to keep her running straight. Then there is broken water all around and wild-looking figures, some naked, rush into the water, seize the boat and haul her up on the beach. Low-voiced greetings and handshakes. They are fellow countrymen, not Japanese.

The cargo is quickly unloaded and you see an astonishing sight. Men with knives and bayonets are hacking open tins of meat and wolfing it down like half-starved dogs. Ponies appear on the beach and are loaded with the supplies you have brought. Figures emerge from the bush and crowd towards the boat. These are the Portuguese men, women and children you have come to rescue. Some, sick and weak, have to be helped. They press around—too many for safety—and more keep climbing in despite your efforts to control them. The boat is already low in the water and still has to get through the surf. At last she is pushed off by the commandos. It is a hard row out to the ship where the human cargo climbs the scrambling net or is lifted on board.

Several trips are made. The turnaround takes ages. After midnight the anchor is in and the engines racing at full power are using 90 gallons every hour of the precious petrol you saved on the slow run in—you fly along at 17 knots with the heavy boat bouncing on a bar-taut line astern. By dawn you hope to be a hundred miles from their airfields.

Daylight reveals a sad sight on the crowded deck with the Portuguese lying around the guns and depth-charge racks in a bad way. Having left all they had in Timor some seem about to leave life itself. They are seasick, vomiting, soaked with spray and lying in their own filth. You wipe their faces and give them tea in chipped mugs.

At last the low brown smudge of Australia's coastline appears on the horizon. You pass through Darwin's boom gate to the Commonwealth Airways' jetty. Army ambulances are waiting. Some Portuguese are carried ashore, some walk, and the Captain lands to report to Operations. You are safe home and can also go ashore . . .

In such operations as in all life, tragedy and comedy stand side by side, and this story would lose something without their mention. Tragedy first . . .

Things were tense on the Timor beach that night. The Japanese were thought to be close. I was standing up to my waist in the low surf beside the boat trying to control it and keep its bow into the waves. We were about to push off, it was already overloaded and I was frightened that we would be swamped. I took a last glance back at the beach, and there standing in the shallows was a tall old man in a white suit and a white panama hat. I can never forget him. He stands there still, motionless, dignified, authoritative. Not calling out to me, beckoning, or making any effort to save himself and come to me. He just stood there looking at the boat and his departing people—just watching us go.

I could not leave him. I waded quickly back and grabbed him. He was very thin and frail, his hair was white, he just looked at me. Neither of us spoke. There was nothing to say. Hampered by my weapons and my soaking, clinging clothes, I dragged him through the surf to the boat, pushed him over the side into the stern sheets beside my oar, jumped in and ordered the commandos to shove off and the sailors to give way. Once we were safely through the surf, I saw the old man turn and look back for a long time at the island in the starlight. Then he took something from his hand, gave it to me and spoke for the first time in elegant English. 'If you go to Portugal show this'. It was a handsome silver ring with a rampant golden lion on a jade green field—perhaps the armorial bearings of some ancient family with centuries of service in the East. Nothing now for him but memories. He had lost everything he had owned on the island except this ring and that he gave away. I did not ask his name and I have never been to Portugal, but I still treasure that moment and his ring.

From Portuguese tragedy to Australian humour. In 1942 when the *Kuru* had been returning from Timor she was attacked for hours by Japanese bombers. There were many moments of great tension while bombs were falling towards her. Once when they exploded all around her she was unscathed, but the boat she had been towing was demolished and the violence of the blasts shook the ship so heavily that her bell rang. The momentary comparative silence that followed was broken by a laconic voice—'Tojo rang the bloody bell—give him a cigar'.

16
The Royal Australian Navy in World War II: A summary

Frank Broeze

This volume arose out of a splendid conference. The authors here open up new areas of study and/or vigorously reassess more 'traditional' subjects and themes, putting them into new contexts. There is much of interest and engagement to be found in this collection both through the advances made in thematic innovation and scholarly analysis and through the immediacy and intimacy of personal experience. One of the greatest challenges for historians is to empathise with, or try to assume the personality and mind-set of, the persons about whom one is writing. However 'detached' academic history writing must be, there will be something vital missing from the account if there is no attempt at historical empathy.

> The attitude of the RAN to historical studies tends to ambivalence. Although the RAN derives from the RN and in tradition, organisation and culture is closely related to it, the RAN has long been uncomfortable with the apparent inconsistencies between much of the naval ethos and the developing Australian identity. This discomfort has been magnified by the fact, that most of the active operations of the RAN were conducted on the basis of integration into the RN's or the USN's operations, without a specific national identity above the level of individual ships or small squadrons.[1]

The paragraph above was written by two Australian naval officers in a recently published review of naval and maritime history. Their comments lead me to make two general comments. First, I firmly hold that naval history is too serious a matter to be left to either civilian or naval historians alone, as both have a vital role to play. One of the most important questions in 'doing' history is: who owns history? Who controls the explanation of the past to the community at large? It cannot be stressed enough that the community comprises all Australians, young–old, male–female, Anglo-Saxon–non-Anglo-Saxon, indigenous and migrant. Naval history needs to be addressed beyond the ranks of the RAN itself and at everyone who does not yet belong to the converted. As long as naval history is being written from within the service, there will always be a problem of communication with the 'outside' world and a hesitation on the part of that outside world to accept both its message and the fact that naval history is part of Australia's mainstream history.

A prime example of the importance of 'open access to history' is given by Bruce Loxton in his riveting reappraisal of the battle of Savo Island. Neither the USN report of the battle, in which the blame for the disaster was squarely put on the shoulders of the RAAF and RAN, nor the relevant documentation was made available to Australia. Knowledge of the battle had, as it were, been hijacked by the Americans in order to protect their own reputation. While this situation relates to a specific and for the RAN particularly harrowing episode in its fighting history, it demonstrates the far more general problems inherent in having a service own and control its own history. There is a very important role to be played by historians from within the service and a healthy naval history profession will never be able to do without them. But all writing should be done with an open and independent mind. Only thus can a true understanding be achieved.

The RAN is an integral part of Australian life, history and heritage. In that context it is particularly appropriate that the conference formed part of the 'Australia Remembers' commemorations, which carried with it the implication that the RAN should be presented in the full context of the national experience and identity. Many references, for example, have been made to the people who served in the RAN in World War II. Two chapters specifically explore the social background of the RAN officer corps and the introduction of female service personnel, but many others contain significant elements of individual or collective biographical approaches. The simple point is that no one is born a naval officer, rating or WRAN. Some, but inevitably only very few, people in the service may have hailed from a naval background, but Australia's naval personnel were, and still are, overwhelmingly of civilian descent. Some may have had yachting backgrounds, others had served in the merchant marine. There were also recruits from Australia's many, and at that stage still populous, port districts. For each of these people the Navy became another avenue to experiencing life at sea or in a maritime institution. But there were also many others who had never had any significant contact with the sea apart from, perhaps, arriving by boat in Australia or enjoying the beach. Let us not forget that by 1939 the 'tall, bronzed, blond, male surf lifesaver' had become perhaps the most powerful icon of Australian contemporary life.

This book shows that naval strategy and operations are still very important and need continually to be reconsidered and reassessed, and also that the time has come to widen the conceptual scope of naval history and to take up the challenge of establishing the connections with the outside world. This outside world, however, is not limited to Australia: naval and maritime history also need their international context, both for comparative purposes and for the perspective

Lieutenant-Commander Leon V. Goldsworthy, GC, DSC, GM, RANVR. Goldsworthy was the RAN's most highly decorated member during the war. He earned an unsurpassed reputation for bravery as a mine disposal expert, working in both the European and Pacific theatres. (AWM 81383)

of 'the other'—whether it be an ally or an enemy. For a full understanding of the RAN one also needs to 'read' its counterparts in Britain, the US, New Zealand, Japan and elsewhere.

Of the subjects brought together in this volume, four deal directly with strategy or with broad strategic issues. Another four discuss specific operations; three of these have strong autobiographical elements. Two are concerned with naval policy and the relationship between the RN and the RAN. One deals with the economic aspects of the RAN in wartime. Two chapters address for the first time social aspects of naval service, and another two are biographical sketches of two outstanding officers. Even more important, however, than this thematic spread is that several of these themes flow over into other chapters. The very personal account by John Betty on the vital pre-invasion work of the RAN Hydrographic Branch, for example, shows a fascinating insight into the wide-ranging connection of Australians with the sea and, at the same time, a part of RAN operations I am sure most historians would never have considered. The same applies very much to Marsden Hordern's moving account of ML *814*'s voyage to Timor. Particularly when East Timor continues to be such a controversial issue in Australia's foreign relations, the emotional elements of the story add a particularly poignant dimension to what is obviously still naval history.

There were also other common factors: the power and excitement of the biographical approach, inter-service rivalry, the relationship of the RAN with its British and American allies and concomitantly the increasing independence of the RAN, the impact of technological change on material, men, tactics and strategy, and the improvisation needed to mobilise the country's fighting resources.

Hordern's story, to indicate another example of cross-fertilisation, throws a particularly interesting light on the issue of resource mobilisation, which is the main subject of Chris Coulthard-Clark and which figures in different ways in many others. Despite its large size, Australia was a country with no more than a small population, a modest economy and only a very limited technological capability. The personnel intake into the RAN, although also circumscribed by political priorities, was ultimately determined by these limiting factors. The same applies to the transformation of the economy for wartime production. Only a few Fairmiles were produced here, against a much larger number of such motor boats in Britain. It was of course not just Australia that was limited in its resources; on a much larger scale the very same applied to Britain, where as Eric Grove argues passionately, some major errors of judgment were made in establishing priorities. As is also emphasised by Coulthard-Clark, much depended on the capability to improvise as industries changed over from the production of peacetime commodities to war *matériel*.

Indeed mobilisation of resources must be related to purpose, quantity and quality. Professionalism went hand in hand with amateurism and the Fairmiles were a classic example of the latter. Although Hordern does not directly question their concept in his story, he vividly describes the apprehension of their crew resulting from their modest maximum speed. Indeed, it is evident that they would have great difficulties successfully fulfilling the functions for which they were designed. Eighteen knots seems dangerously insufficient for the Timor dashes. The answer, given in the conference discussion, to questions with regard to the performance of the Fairmiles in combat with German E-boats in the Channel, left no room for doubt about their deficiencies.

The Timor dashes and the hydrographic work of the RAN, which interestingly was determined by the movements of the American reconquest of the Philippines rather than the Australian landings in Borneo, add significantly to the picture of Australia's naval efforts in World War II. The overall pattern of these operations is impressively set out in the incisive and revisionist five-stage account by James Goldrick. For many, however, the chapters that open most new insights will probably be those by David Stevens on the Australian convoy work in the SWPA and by Ian Cowman on US strategy decision-making, in which is explained that the area came about as a result of a personal decision by US President Roosevelt. Badgered by the Australian Government, Roosevelt intervened with his own military in order to establish the strategic lines on the map which delineated the SWPA. Within that area the convoy work done by the RAN has for a very long time been totally overlooked. Stevens makes the very important point that the exercise of seapower rests not only in the preparation for and (hopefully) successful fighting of sea battles. Especially for Australia, whose combat naval effort was inevitably modest and hardly ever independent, to keep the sea and to control the sea lines of communications was perhaps the single most important service that could be rendered to the Allied strategic cause. Stevens' chapter also reminds us that the overall largest contribution made by Australia in the war against Japan was probably its very existence and location, that is, its availability as the base from which the conquest of South-East Asia could be mounted and supplied. It was exactly the safeguarding of that thrust northwards, first to New Guinea and then to the Dutch East Indies and the Philippines, that the convoy system of the SWPA was set to ensure. This emphasised the importance of the failure of the IJN to cut off communications between the US and Australia, and equally, its failure to establish sea control in the Indian Ocean. An aspect still requiring further research is the use of Australian ports as staging posts for convoys from the American west coast to Iran and the Soviet Union.

Several authors reassess Australia's wartime naval operations, strategy and strategic environment. Australia's engagement in the European theatre is summed up in Grove's hard-hitting and questioning chapter which, besides describing the RAN's efforts in sharp relief, raises the question of Britain's strategic and political priorities. Although not immediately acceptable for Australian ears, now almost saturated with the new orthodoxy of Britain's 'betrayal' of Australia and New Zealand through the anti-Japanese bluff of the Singapore strategy, strong points are made about the Admiralty's desire for an appeasement with Italy and the sending of a 'real' naval force to Singapore. Even as late as the second half of 1941, Grove argues, Britain's priorities could have been rearranged, in terms of both sea and air power in order to strengthen the defence of the British Empire in the 'East'. Not having done so, it was agreed that the sending of Force 'Z' (not the only time Churchill willingly sacrificed life for political purpose) had more to do with the as yet uncertain relationship with the US than a realistic strategy to halt the southern Japanese onslaught.

The relationship with the US and the general strategic environment of Australia in World War II are expertly discussed by Ian Cowman and Joe Straczek, respectively. These chapters show the vital necessity of seeing and understanding 'the larger picture' and the importance at the highest level of planning and strategy-making of the political dimension. In fact, there is hardly a chapter in this volume in which politics do not crop up in one way or another, but its most dramatic manifestations are no doubt at the points where decisions about the largest concentrations of resources were made. From the Australian viewpoint, these decisions related to the extraordinary and extraordinarily wasteful, double-barrelled US Pacific strategy and the division of the northward reconquest into the US campaign against the Philippines and the Australian 'sideshow' in Borneo.

David Brown adds significantly to our understanding of the last phases of the war through his discussion of the establishment (and somewhat pathetic failure to arrive on time) of the BPF and its quest for bases in Australia; whatever came of the latter, the BFP certainly discovered 'total hospitality'. Once more political reasons abounded in the British Government's decision to reassign naval power after VE-Day from the Atlantic to the Far East. Highly interesting aspects of this are the search for suitable bases in Australia for the BPF and its adoption of the American 'fleet train' method which resulted in a relatively very high 'tooth to tail' ratio.

The BPF began to arrive at a stage when, through necessity rather than by design, the RAN had significantly broken the RN mould, in which from its inception it had been cast. Alastair Cooper gives a comprehensive overview of the many and varied connections between the RN and the Australian service suggesting that the experiences of World War II hastened, but by no means established, the true independence of the RAN. Indeed he makes it clear that investigating and evaluating the influence of the RAN—an influence also vividly evidenced by Jason Sears—means the drawing up of a balance sheet with a strikingly complex set of entries and accounts. In hindsight we know that the RAN, after the wartime period of close cooperation with the USN, would once again orient itself towards Britain, especially in the matter of naval aviation, but it became evident that the pre-1941 imitation and adulation of the RN could never again be established. Of the two biographical chapters, Tony Grazebrook on the late Vice-Admiral John Collins, provides a highly individual and fascinating window onto the gradual emancipation of the RAN within the complex formal and informal network that tied it to the RN; equally, the various stages of Collins' career illustrate the overall Imperial relationship between Australia and Britain.

Barbara Winter's chapter on Commander Long, from its twilight atmosphere, casts another set of spotlights on both naval work and the Imperial connection. Much of Long's work, apart from his setting up the coastwatcher system, was entirely unknown and its sheer span and importance will come as a revelation to most readers. Winter's remarkable determination and research skills found here a most thankful theme to pursue. As we now know, naval intelligence is no longer the field of people with persecution complexes or conspiracy fixations. Indeed it is no longer possible to write naval history of any kind without taking the dimensions of gathering intelligence and covert action into consideration. Quite apart from their intrinsic importance in influencing decisions they can add profoundly to the collective experiences and mythology of Australia's people as the exploits of Fairmiles in the Timor Sea eloquently show.

Chris Coulthard-Clark's pioneering and perceptive account of the mobilisation of Australia's economic resources provides an entirely new dimension to our

Labuan Island, Borneo, 10 June 1945. Landing craft preparing to disembark troops while the cruiser USS Phoenix *bombards Japanese shore installations. The photo was taken from the Landing Ship Infantry (LSI) HMAS* Westralia. Westralia *was converted from an armed merchant cruiser during 1943 and together with two other Australian LSI's,* Kanimbla *and* Manoora, *she took part in seven amphibious assaults in New Guinea, the Philippines and Borneo. (AWM 107014)*

understanding of Australia's naval effort. More than in any other area drastic changes had to be made in order to adapt Australian life to the requirements of wartime. Although the general story of the transformation of the economy is relatively well known, no specific studies of the naval dimension had yet been made. As it turned out the resulting picture is greatly varied. The economic and technological base from which the government had to start was remarkably narrow, but improvisation led to some extraordinary achievements. At all turns too there were manpower problems, partly because of the small size of the remaining workforce in Australia, partly because of the conflicting demands of other industries, partly also because of the remarkable extent of strikes and other industrial problems. The most immediate priority was the large-scale expansion of repair facilities, but explosives, heavy ordnance, mines, torpedoes and, above all, radar and sonar were produced in sometimes remarkably large quantities. The RAN worked up to an unprecedented degree of self-reliance which would have long-term consequences in terms of spin-offs to the post-war civilian economy and the way naval planners and others thought about Australia's identity; even so, in terms of large vessels and material Australia remained largely dependent on imports and, in particular, supply conditions in Britain.

One of the major themes linking virtually all chapters is how much the RAN and all its personnel stood under enormous constraints. There were financial, economic, administrative, demographic, geographic and, ultimately, political constraints. Politicians could make positive but also negative contributions. Almost nowhere can the political angle be neglected as politicians and politics will always intrude. The same applies to ideology, the social belief systems of those in power. These ranged from views on the suitability of women for wartime service and Catholic working-class men as officers, to the relative professional capabilities and courage of Anglo-Saxon warriors and their Japanese counterparts.

There is one other element that has never figured largely in Australian naval history but which makes a tantalising appearance in two or three anecdotal episodes: the role of the press. During World War II Australians did not get their news unadulterated. The government watched carefully what information could be entrusted to readers and largely dictated what the papers could carry. But the press generally does not mediate between government and the reading public in a passive way; on the contrary, it takes a mostly active role in shaping or even creating what is called 'the news'. Kathryn Spurling referred to the depiction of the WRANs in the male-dominated press, either as 'Mae Wests' or 'spinsters'—a rather amazing version of Anne Summers' suggestion that women were either 'damned whores or God's police'. One of the biggest issues that women volunteers had to fight was for the destruction of complex and deeply ingrained prejudice. This phenomenon was not singular to World War II but the backwardness of the RAN on this issue of recognising the value of women stood in sharp contrast to the attitude of the Army and Air Force. In a more general sense what this episode shows is that, in its relationship with the Australian people, the RAN had to realise that the press is an extremely powerful image-maker. The very public power of the press barons in turn leaves the newspaper editors open to be used by ambitious and clever people. Grazebrook pointedly refers to Vice-Admiral Collins' astute awareness of the importance of public relations. The media are there to be used by those who understand their power.

I stress the importance of the press, because often, when it comes to making decisions between allocating funds to the Navy, the Army or the Air Force, or giving priority to defence rather than to hospitals, the Navy does not automatically rank. Public awareness of what a navy is and what it does has remained underdeveloped. This is a lesson that applies as much to the 1990s as the 1930s and 1940s. The crucial concept here is something I would like to refer to as 'maritime ideology', the attitude of the community at large to the importance of the sea for Australia. It is only within the terms of that relationship that the people can properly understand the role of the RAN and what it should and can do for the country. Both historically and currently there still lies a great task ahead.

In the context of linking the past and the present both Coulthard-Clark and Goldrick raise an extremely important issue related to the previous points: what impact did World War II have on Australia after 1945? Goldrick makes very clear that the last period of the war was very much concerned with planning for the post-war world. Wartime industrialisation, similarly, could not but have important economic and demographic consequences for the future. As Cooper reminds us, questions as to how the war affected people and institutions and, for example, the relationship between the RN and the RAN are extremely complex. Moreover, for an investigation of such issues one cannot stop in 1945. In many cases, for a proper perspective the story needs to be carried on till 1995, next year to 1996, and so on. History never stops and the impact of such dramatic events as World War II can only be understood in the very long term. It would be deplorably short-sighted if the general interest in World War II came to an end with the expiration of the 'Australia Remembers' year. It needs to be carried on with both a scholarly and a personal sense of commitment. It would also be a great pity, if only the war years were studied and not their impact on the post-1945 period.

Indeed I feel somewhat uncomfortable with the fact that the conference was held mainly because it happened to be fifty years ago that World War II ended. In principle there is nothing against a national program like 'Australia Remembers', especially not as the timespan involved is short enough to have large numbers of veterans present to add their personal experiences and testimony to that of the written records of the time. History, however, nowadays tends to be run by the tyranny of the round figure. From 1996, World War II and Australia's effort will no longer be a neat fifty years ago and suddenly it will disappear from the public face of the earth, probably until the year 2045. Yet, for historians and veterans alike, nothing will change: all that has been will retain the same intrinsic significance.

What this means is that we should not think to stop our work at the end of 1995 but firmly fix our eyes on the agenda for future research. This volume is splendid in terms of what has been achieved. Major steps forward have been made since the more general 1989 conference whose proceedings were published under the title *Reflections on the RAN*.[2] But it is also clear that much remains to be done. It is inevitable that in a book this size not all themes can be discussed. Many gaps remain to be filled and, equally importantly, much of the received wisdom in other areas needs to be scrutinised in the light of fuller documentation that is now available and the different understanding of the world that our passing through 'interesting' times brings with it. There is virtually no area in the history of the RAN in World War II and by extension during its entire existence that is not capable of being reassessed. Goldrick's work on naval policy, or that of Cooper on the relationship with the RN, are prime examples of how much revisionism is needed and where it will lead. The same applies to what appears to be one of the most commonly publicised aspects on the Navy—its active service record. Grove and Loxton demonstrate that individual operations too are still subject to revision.

The surrender of Vice-Admiral M. Kamada, IJN, Commander 22 Naval Base Force, on board the River class frigate HMAS Burdekin *off Balikpapan, Borneo on 8 September 1945. Surrender ceremonies would continue to take place in RAN vessels until October. (AWM 115823)*

Then there are many aspects that as yet have hardly been touched on. Coulthard-Clark has emphasised the need for a thorough understanding of the economic elements of the nation's naval war effort. The financial sides have hardly been touched upon and the great (and clearly even nowadays still divisive) issue of the waterfront must also be tackled. Social history has been introduced to us through the innovative and fascinating accounts by Spurling and Sears. But despite or perhaps maybe because of their pioneering work, it is evident that they have done little more than show us the tip of the iceberg. For their specific populations more can be done and there are of course several other maritime groups that as yet have been totally overlooked—for example, naval wives and families, the epitome of the home front.

Betty's autobiographical account and even more so the chapters by Winter and Grazebrook show the unique and great value of a biography as means to open windows on the past. Some naval biographies have been written but many—both individual and collective—are needed. Biography has for some time not been in vogue with professional historians, but it is making a very strong comeback as the realisation has been reawakened that it can add enormously to our understanding of history. Besides the two specifically biographical chapters there are many others in this collection that highlight the opinions, decisions and deeds of individuals. Many of them would warrant a full-scale biography. With such analytical, rather than purely narrative, studies we would understand so much more of the overall institutions, operations, policies, decisions and so on in which these people were involved. One of the most interesting projects could combine many of the issues raised previously: a full biographical and icono-graphical study of the official war artist, Frank Norton.

The larger picture needs to be adopted as well, which would ultimately add up to 'maritime ideology': the RAN in the Australian economy, in Australian society, and—as was referred to in the earlier quotation—in the Australian identity. These are subjects that have hardly been discussed at all until now. The RAN is by nature, as are many comparable institutions, inward looking. Most people interested in naval history work inside the Navy. The great challenge is to explain the RAN's role and Australia's naval effort within the total context of both Australia and World War II in general. A fuller understanding also involves the making of comparisons. I very much agree with historians who hold that history cannot be 'true history' if it is not comparative. Judicious assessments can only be made within a full context and by comparison. The problem for the RAN is with which service or country to compare it. With Canada? That has often been done, but the situation there was quite different. Britain? The RN was hardly the equal of the RAN. New Zealand? Can it be relevant? I firmly believe, yes! If naval history, or maritime history in general, is approached thematically, it can be done and then almost any comparison can be enlightening. It is extremely useful and worthwhile comparing one's own service with one's allies and opponents, learning to view issues from their viewpoints. Conversely there is no reason why Australians could not tell others what an Australian view on the RN or USN has to offer. Maybe such a view might not be popular but it is important that in this way a truly international exchange of ideas and views is established.

To finish, I should like to stress the stimulating quality of the innovative and invigorating chapters offered here. But the stimulus should not be allowed to evaporate. The enthusiasm and commitment should be maintained in a future program of conferences, research and publication. The latter should be carried out on several levels of scholarly studies, general trade books, popular publications, museum guides and especially displays-—that, after all, is the medium through which most Australians see and 'read' their history. Further attempts should be made to introduce a naval dimension into the primary and high school curricula. In most states several alternative avenues, such as units or sections on Australia in World War II or the Cold War, already exist.

I also think that the Australian Navy is mature and important enough to warrant a systematic production of monographs and documentary volumes. One possibility for a theme would be the personal papers of prominent officers— where the first candidates to suggest themselves would be Collins and Farncomb. Volumes could also be related to specific issues or a specific period within the general context of, for example, strategy-making or the acquisition of new weapon systems like aircraft carriers, frigates or submarines. There would be many ways in which one could bring together a collection of sources that would be useful and enlightening for a larger audience than the single historian. One could think about a Frank Norton volume, with text and illustrations. Every reader could then, as it were, have a look into the historical kitchen and make up their own minds and opinions. No individual or group would 'own' this past. And this would also produce marvellous material for courses in or dealing with naval history which I hope will gradually become available throughout the country. I am not overly optimistic on that point but I would like to suggest that a vision of simultaneously introducing courses and making resources material available should be our beacon for the future.

Notes

Chapter 1 Australian naval policy 1939–45

1 R. Hyslop, *Aye Aye, Minister*, AGPS, Canberra, 1990, p. 6.
2 P. Hasluck, *The Government and the People 1939–41*, AWM, Canberra, 1952, p. 443.
3 VADM J.W. Durnford, 'A Shellback Remembers', unpublished, IWM, p. 210.
4 Committee of Imperial Defence Paper no. 837, Feb. 1939, CAB 53/44, PRO.
5 *The Navy List,* Oct. 1939 and Jan. 1945, Government Printer, Melbourne, gives breakdowns of the naval staff organisation; also H. Burrell, *Mermaids Do Exist*, Macmillan, Melbourne, 1986, p. 73.
6 Memo. ACNS to Minister for Defence, 29 Aug. 1939, CRS A2671 14/1939, AA.
7 G. H. Gill, *The RAN 1939–45*, vol. I, AWM, Canberra, 1957, p. 64.
8 D.M. Horner, *High Command*, Allen & Unwin, Sydney, 1982, p. 27; cable PM to High Com. in London, 1 Feb. 1940, in *Documents on Australian Foreign Policy 1937–49* (DAFP), vol. III, AGPS, Canberra, p. 79.
9 Minutes, Council of Defence, 24 Feb. 1938, CRS 1971/216, AA.
10 J. Collins, *As Luck Would Have It,* Angus & Robertson, Sydney, 1965, p. 70.
11 B.N. Primrose, 'Equipment and Naval Policy 1919–42' in *Australian Journal of Politics and History*, vol. XXII, no. 2, 1977, p. 166.
12 War Cabinet Minute 325, 11 Jun. 1940, DAFP, vol. III, pp. 407–8; Horner, p. 35.
13 Gill, vol. I, p. 250.
14 ibid., p. 118.
15 A.J. Marder, *Old Friends, New Enemies*, vol. I, Clarendon Press, Oxford, 1981, p. 79.
16 Cable, Acting PM to SecState for Dominion Affairs, 12 Feb. 1941, DAFP vol. IV, pp. 382–4.
17 Gill, vol. I, p. 269.
18 Admiral Sir Ragnar Colvin, *Memoirs*, Wintershill publications, Durley, 1992, p. 127.
19 Marder, vol. I, p. 208.
20 Letter, Admiralty to Treasury, 8 Aug. 1941, ADM 1/134687, PRO.
21 Colvin, p. 130.
22 Marder, vol. I, pp. 213–42.

23 Gill, vol. I, p. 461.
24 T. Frame, *HMAS Sydney,* Hodder & Stoughton, Sydney, 1993, p. 9.
25 Churchill to Curtin, 3 Jan. 1942, ADM 205/10, PRO; Marder, vol. I, p. 27.
26 R. Bell, *Unequal Allies,* Melbourne University Press, Melbourne, 1977.
27 B. Loxton with C. Coulthard-Clark, *The Shame of Savo*, Allen & Unwin, Sydney, 1994, p. 255.
28 Collins, p. 133.
29 Air Vice-Marshal J.E. Hewitt, *Adversity in Success*, Langate, Melbourne, 1980, p. 256, gives Hewitt's record of a 1944 visit to a USN escort carrier.
30 Letter, Admiral Sir James Somerville (CinC Eastern Fleet) to Admiral of the Fleet Sir Andrew Cunningham (First Sea Lord), 27 Jun. 1942. The author is indebted to Professor Michael Simpson for this and other material in the Cunningham and Somerville papers.
31 Gill, vol. II, p. 244.
32 Letter, Colvin to Foley, 9 May 1944, Foley Papers, AWM.
33 H.P. Willmott, 'The Evolution of British Strategy in the War Against Japan', in *Reflections on the RAN*, eds T. Frame, J. Goldrick, P. Jones, Kangaroo Press, Kenthurst, 1991, p. 180.
34 J. Goldrick, 'Selections from the Memoirs and Correspondence of Captain James Bernard Foley CBE, RAN', in *The Naval Miscellany Volume V*, ed. N.A.M. Rodger, Navy Records Society, London, 1984. pp. 521–2.
35 Letter, Royle to Cunningham, 25 Mar. 1944, Cunningham Papers, Add. MSS 52572, British Museum.
36 Willmott, pp. 181–2.
37 Request for return of RAN Loan Personnel, ADM 1/12559, PRO.
38 J. Goldrick, 'Carriers for the Commonwealth', in *Reflections on the RAN*, p. 224; Horner, p. 371; A. Wright, *Australian Carrier Decisions*, Department of Defence 1978, p. 46.
39 Wright, pp. 50–1.
40 Goldrick, 'Carriers for the Commonwealth', p. 217.
41 Wright, p. 60.
42 Minute, Chancellor of the Exchequer to PM, 11 Apr. 1945, ADM 1/18140, PRO.
43 Wright, p. 74.
44 Gill, vol. II, p. 472.
45 CPD House of Representatives: PM's Statement on Defence Policy, 23 March 1945.
46 Letters, Royle to Colvin, 28 Dec. 1944, Royle to Foley, 20 Jan. 1945, Foley to Royle 17 Feb. 1945, Foley Papers.
47 At least five more enemy submarines were sunk by RN ships under the command of RANR or RANVR officers. Figures have not been computed for British units under the command of permanent RAN officers on exchange.
48 Letter, Parker to Foley, 12 Apr. 1945, Foley Papers.

Chapter 2   The Pacific War: A strategic overview

1 M.P. Parillo, 'The IJN in WWII', in *Reevaluating Major Naval Combatants of WWII*, ed. J. Sadkovich, Greenwood Press, NY, 1990, p. 63.

2 RADM Y. Hirama, 'Japanese Naval Preparations for WWII', *Naval War College Review*, Spring 1991, p. 75.

3 I. Hata, 'Admiral Yamamoto and the Japanese Navy', in *From Pearl Harbor to Hiroshima*, ed. S. Dockrill, MacMillan Press, London, 1994, p. 64.

4 US Strategic Bombing Survey (Pacific), *The Campaigns of the Pacific War*, Washington, 1946, p. 3.

5 M. Fuchida & M. Okumiya, *Midway*, USNI Press, Annapolis, 1992, p. 72.

6 CID E.4, 'Empire Naval Policy and Co-operation', Feb. 1921, p. 6, AWM124 74/24.

7 Though historically described as the 'Singapore Strategy', the naval base was only one part of a worldwide strategy.

8 'Empire Naval Policy and Co-operation', p. 12.

9 ibid., p. 11.

10 T. Ishimura, *Japan Must Fight Britain*, Paternoster Library, London, 1937, p. 142.

11 'Conference at Penang between the CinCs of the China, East Indies and Australia Stations' 7 Mar. 1921, MP1587 311J, AA.

12 Admiralty letters, 29 Jan. 1924, Jan. 1938. War Memoranda (Eastern), p. 17, AWM124.

13 ibid.

14 S.W. Kirby, *History of the Second World War: The War With Japan*, vol. I, HMSO, London, 1957, p. 17.

15 J.R. Leutze, *Bargaining For Supremacy*, University of North Carolina Press, Chapel Hill, 1977, p. 16.

16 ibid., p. 27.

17 *Ships of the Royal Navy: Statement of Losses*, HMSO, London, 1947.

18 During 1939–41, three battleships, four aircraft carriers, sixteen cruisers, 88 destroyers and 42 submarines were built. M.M. Postan, *British War Production*, HMSO, London, 1952, p. 133.

19 C. Barnett, *Engage the Enemy More Closely*, Hodder & Stoughton, London, 1991, p. 381.

20 Kirby, p. 18.

21 Message, Admiralty to CinC Ceylon, 19 Mar. 1942, MP1185/8 1932/2/261, AA.

22 P. Kennedy, *The War Plans of the Great Powers 1880–1914*, Unwin Hyman, London, 1988, p. 35.

23 L. Morton, *Strategy and Command*, Department of Army, Washington, 1962, p. 27.

24 ibid.

25 'Overall Plan for the Defeat of Japan', CCS 417, 2 Dec. 1943, p. 1.

26 ibid., p.2.

27 J. Winton, *The Forgotten Fleet*, Douglas-Boyd Books, Sussex, 1989, p. 18.

28 E. S. Miller, *War Plan Orange*, USNI Press, Annapolis, 1991, p. 333.

Chapter 3   Forging an alliance? The American naval commitment to the South Pacific, 1940–42

1 Memo., DNI to CNO, 31 May 1923, GB 409; memo. SecWar to SecState, 28 Dec. 1923, 811.014/96, RG 59, NA.

2 'Lessons of the Hawaii War Game', *Literary Digest*, 23 May 1925, pp. 14–15.

3 Memo., 'The Utility of Christmas Island from the Strategic Standpoint', DWPD to

CNO, 23 Jan. 1926, GB 414; memo. SecNav to SecState, 30 Jan. 1926, 811.014/123, RG 59, NA.

4 Memo., F. D. R. to Leahy, 30 Jul. 1937, 811.0141, PG/12.5, RG 59, NA.

5 Telegram, Lindsay to FO, 17 Feb. 1939, pt. V, AVIA. 2/1994, PRO.

6 Telegram, High Com. NZ to DO, 30 Mar. 1939, ibid.

7 Telegram, High Com. Western Pacific to SS for Colonies, 19 Jul. 1939; Letter, Acheson to Balfour, 13 Sep. 1939 ; 'Observations on US claims to 23 Pacific Islands hitherto regarded as British', report by FO, 16 Nov. 1939, pt. VI, ibid.

8 Letter, Acheson to Balfour, 13 Sep. 1939, ibid.

9 Message, OPNAV to CINCPAC, 14 Dec. 1941, CINCPAC Greybook, p. 50, NHD.

10 Message, 301740 COMINCH to CINCPAC, 31 Dec. 1941, ibid. p. 121.

11 B.M. Simpson, *Admiral Harold R. Stark*, University of South Carolina, Colombia, 1989, pp. 2–4.

12 Memo., McDowell to Coleridge, 20 Dec. 1941, CAB 122/1055, PRO; Telegram, Casey to Curtin and Evatt, 16 Dec. 1941, Doc. 204, in *Documents on Australian Foreign Policy*, (DAFP), vol. V, ed. R.G. Neale, AGPS, Canberra, 1976, p. 325.

13 C. Glover, *Command Performance—With Guts!*, Greenwich, NY, 1969, p. 32; H. Sanders, 'King of the Navy' in *USNIP*, Aug. 1974, p. 57.

14 E.J. King & W. M. Whitehill, *Fleet Admiral King*, W.W. Norton, NY, 1952, p. 373.

15 Telegram, JSM to COS, 18 Feb. 1942, CAB 122/198, PRO.

16 Message, 191815, COMINCH to CINCPAC, 19 Jan. 1942, Greybook, p. 178; for details on US expansion across the Pacific, M. Matloff, *Strategic Planning for Coalition Warfare 1941–42*, USGPO, Washington, 1953, pp. 114–19, 147.

17 D. Van der Vat, *The Pacific Campaign*, Simon and Schuster, NY, 1991, p. 209.

18 A.D. Chandler, ed., *The Papers of Dwight D. Eisenhower*, John Hopkins, Baltimore, 1970, p. 151.

19 Sir John Slessor, *The Central Blue*, Cassell, London, 1956, p. 494.

20 L.H. Morton, *Strategy and Command*, USGPO, Washington, 1962, p. 218.

21 D. MacArthur, *Reminiscences*, Heinemann, London, 1964, p. 183.

22 Minutes, Arcadia 9th Meeting, 11 Jan. 1942, Item 4, CAB 88/1; memo. 'Security of Island Bases between Hawaii and Australia', CMDR R.E. Libby to King, 2 Jan. 1942, King Papers, ABC4/1–4/9, NHD.

23 Cable, Curtin to Casey, 1 Jan. 1942, Doc. 247, DAFP, pp. 396–8.

24 76th Congress, *Pearl Harbor Attack Hearings*, USGPO, Washington, 1946, pt. 15, pp. 1516, 1533.

25 CCS 1st Meeting, 23 Jan. 1942, Item 2, Records of the CCS & JCS, RG 218, NA. CAB 88/1, PRO.

26 Memo., 'Changes in ABDA–ANZAC Areas evolving from Developments in the Far East', by King, 17 Feb. 1942, CCS 381, Section 1 (1–24–42); CCS 5th Meeting, 17 Feb. 1942, Item 1, ibid.

27 Cable, Churchill to Curtin, 12 Jan. 1942, Doc. 271, pp. 432–34; Cable, Evatt to Casey, 22 Jan. 1942, Doc. 291, DAFP, pp. 458–9.

28 Appreciation by Australia and New Zealand, 1 Mar. 1942 , A2670, 118/1942, AA.

29 The proposal to link ABDA and ANZAC seems to have come from RADM Turner. 'Recommended new Strategic Deployment against Japan', 17 Feb. 1942, CNO/WPD Papers, A16-3(4) POA, NHD.

30 JCS 5th Meeting, 9 Mar. 1942, Item 1, Records of the CCS & JCS.

31 MacArthur's name was put forward as a potential commander of a combined defence area in December 1941. Cable, Casey to Dept. External Affairs, 21 Dec. 1941, A3300, 101, AA.

32 Morton, p. 248.

33 'Summary of Status with Respect to Spheres of Strategic Responsibility', 30 Mar. 1942, Double Zero Files, King Papers, NHC.

34 T. Buell, *Master of Sea Power*, Little Brown, Boston, 1980, p. 193.

35 Message, CINCPAC to COMINCH 092245, 5 Feb. 1942 ; CINCPAC, 21 Feb. 1942, Greybook.

36 E.B. Potter, *Nimitz*, USNI Press, Annapolis, 1976, p. 41.

37 J.B. Lundstrom, *The First South Pacific Campaign*, USNI Press, Annapolis, 1976, pp. 29–33.

38 E.P. Hoyt, *How They Won the War in the Pacific*, Weybright & Talley, 1970, NY, p. 134.

39 Buell, p. 219.

40 S.E. Morison, *History of USN Operations in WWII*, vol. 5, Little Brown, Boston, 1948–62, p. 315.

41 W.R. Braisted, *The USN in the Pacific, 1909–22*, University of Texas, Austin, 1971; E.S. Miller, *War Plan Orange*, USNI Press, Annapolis, 1991.

42 The 1913 plan asked for a period of two to three months; by 1924 an indeterminate period longer than three months; by 1936 two to three years. 'Naval War Plan Orange', microfilm 2, *Strategic Planning in the USN—Its Evolution and Execution*, Scholarly Resources Inc., Wilmington, undated; L. Morton, 'War Plan "Orange": Evolution of a Strategy', *World Politics*, vol. 2, Jan. 1959, pp. 221–50.

43 Dyer, vol. 2, pp. 252–3.

44 Telegram, BAD to ADM, 25 Jan. 1942, CAB 122/185, PRO. When CAPT H.W. Hill from the Navy's War Plans Division was called to Washington in 1940 to make a presentation on War Plan 'Orange', he was dismayed at the negative reaction of the Bureau chiefs. Given the budgetary limitations, most of them saw his ideas as impractical. The single exception was Admiral King, who chastised his brother officers for their 'lack of offensive spirit.' Hoyt, p.3.

45 Message, COMINCH to CINCPAC and ComSoPac, 020235, 1 Dec. 1942, COMINCH Files, NHD.

46 Memo., 'Strategic Deployment of US Forces for 1943', by King, 13 Mar. 1943, CCS 381 (2–8–43), Section 1, RG 418, NA.

47 ibid.

48 General Arnold, *Global Mission*, Hutchinson, London, 1951, p. 249.

Chapter 4   The effect of World War II on RAN–RN relations

1 J. Grey, *A Military History of Australia*, Cambridge University Press (CUP), Cambridge, 1990, p. 77.

2 Evidence of the extent to which the RAN was melded with the RN is widespread. Some examples are War Cabinet Agendum no. 165/1945, 'Naval Construction in Australia', CRS A816/1, 40/301/540, AA; Statement Relating to [UK] Defence by the UK PM and Minister for Defence, Feb. 1946, CTS A5954, 1634/1, AA;

J. Goldrick, 'Selections from the Memoirs and Correspondence of CAPT J.B. Foley, RAN' in *The Naval Miscellany, Vol. 5*, ed. N.A.H. Roger, Navy Records Society, London; Foley Papers, AWM.

3 D. Zimmerman, 'The RAN and the RCN and High Technology in the Second World War' in *Reflections on the RAN*, eds T. Frame, J. Goldrick, P. Jones, Kangaroo Press, Kenthurst, 1991.

4 B.N. Primrose, 'Equipment and Naval Policy 1919–42', *Australian Journal of Politics and History*, Aug. 1977, pp. 166–8.

5 D.P. Mellor, *Australia in the War of 1939–45: The Role of Science and Industry*, AWM, Canberra, 1958, pp. 453–80.

6 ibid.

7 Defence Committee Minute No. 269/1944, 18 Aug. 1944; War Cabinet Agendum 55/1945, CRS A2670, AA.

8 E. Grove, *From Vanguard to Trident*, The Bodley Head, London, 1987, pp. 18–19.

9 Correspondence during 1945 relating to the transfer of vessels to the RAN, DO35/1681, PRO.

10 Letter, Foley (RAN Liaison Officer in London) to Royle, 1 May 1945, Foley Papers.

11 Letter, Foley to Royle, 12 Mar. Foley Papers; letter, Admiral Sir Louis Hamilton, RN (First Naval Member) to Admiral Sir A.B. Cunningham, RN (First Sea Lord), 2 Aug. 1945, Cunningham Papers.

12 Letter, Foley to Hamilton, 2 May 1946, Foley Papers.

13 Letter, Hamilton to Admiral Sir John Cunningham, RN (First Sea Lord), 27 Nov. 1947, ADM205/69, PRO.

14 Letter, Royle to Foley, 23 May 1944, Foley Papers.

15 Letter, CNS to Minister for the Navy, 28 May 1947, CRS A5954, 1649/1, AA; letter, Hamilton to Foley, 4 Oct. 1946, Foley Papers.

16 Defence Committee Agenda 13/1946, Jan. 1946, CRS A5799/1, 13/46, AA.

17 The 'Q' class were transferred in preference to the 'N' class, which the RAN had also manned during the war, because their superior sea-keeping qualities and greater endurance better suited them to the RAN's needs. Letter, CAPT(S) C.A. Parker, RAN to Foley, 23 May 1944, Foley Papers.

18 Although the RAN built some ships at Cockatoo Dockyard in Sydney, this did not yield much experience, as many of its middle-ranking and senior officers were RN loan. As a result much of the experience gained would have been repatriated to the RN.

19 I.J. Cunningham, *Work Hard, Play Hard*, AGPS, Canberra, 1988, gives many insights into the alignment of RAN officer training with the RN.

20 A. Cooper, 'At the Crossroads: Anglo–Australian Naval Relations 1945–71', *The Journal of Military History*, Oct. 1994, pp. 710–14.

21 Primrose, pp. 166–7.

22 *The Navy List*, 1937–47, AWM. Analysis is based on figures for officers, however it is likely that trends would be the same for sailors.

23 W.A.B. Douglas, 'Conflict and Innovation in the RCN, 1939–45', in *Naval Warfare in the Twentieth Century 1900–45*, ed. G. Jordan, Croom Helm, London, 1977.

24 Letter, Pearce (Minister for Defence) to Brigadier General McNicoll, 17 Nov. 1933, Foley Papers.

25 Memo., Royle to Minister for the Navy, 13 Dec. 1943, Foley Papers.

26 When Crutchley gave up command of TG 74 it was split into RN and USN Task Groups.

27 Memo., Royle to Minister for the Navy, 23 Feb. 1944, Foley Papers.

28 Letter, Hamilton to RADM C.B. Barry (Naval Secretary to the First Lord), 4 Apr. 1946, ibid.

29 Letter, Hamilton to VADM McGrigor (RN VCNS), 12 Jun. 1946, ibid.

30 Correspondence relating to communications in the BPF, Nov. 1945, CRS MP 1049/5, 2037/2/2044, AA; R. Humble, *Fraser of North Cape*, Routledge & Keegan Paul, London, 1983, pp. 249–50.

31 Minute, DTSR to DCNS, 23 Jan. 1947, held by author.

32 Letters, Foley to Captain (S) C.A. Parker, 7 Aug. and 27 Dec. 1945, Foley Papers.

33 Letter, Royle to Foley, 23 May 1944, ibid.

34 J. Goldrick, 'Carriers for the Commonwealth', in *Reflections on the RAN*, pp. 222–6.

Chapter 5   The contribution of industry to Navy's war in the Pacific

1 *Age* (Melbourne), 30 Oct. 1943.

2 Minute, E. Herbert, Assistant Works Manager of Ordnance Factory Maribyrnong, to M.M. O'Loughlin, Divisional Manager of Ordnance Factories, 20 Nov. 1943; records at ADI Footscray facility, Victoria.

3 AWM, 19 Aug. 1994. To some extent sales were directly related to the length of time that volumes had been available to the public, with the best sellers (Army-I and Air-III) among the first published in the 1950s. This is not the whole story, however, as the Civil-II volume (*Government and the People 1942–45*) had outsold Mellor even though it did not appear until 1970!

4 Cockatoo Docks & Engineering Co. Pty Ltd, *Cockatoo Docks, Sydney: War Record 1939–45*, undated, p. 42; D.P. Mellor, *The Role of Science and Industry*, AWM, Canberra, 1958, pp. 463–4.

5 *Cockatoo Docks . . . War Record*, pp. 38, 40.

6 ibid. pp. 58, 64.

7 ibid. p. 8.

8 ibid. p. 17.

9 R.G. Parker, *Cockatoo Island*, Nelson, Melbourne, 1977, p. 46.

10 Mellor, pp. 453–9.

11 Parker, p. 46; *Cockatoo Docks . . . War Record*, pp. 23, 30; Mellor, p. 457.

12 Department of Munitions, *A summary of the Development of Munitions Production in Australia, 1940–45* (reprinted from *Official Year Book of the Commonwealth of Australia*, no.36: 1944–45, Canberra, 1947) p. 1061.

13 ibid.

14 Parker, p. 50; *Cockatoo Docks . . . War Record*, pp. 60–2, 66, 68.

15 Parker, pp. 47, 49–50; *Cockatoo Docks . . . War Record*, pp. 44, 46, 48, 52, 70.

16 Parker, p. 47.

17 Mellor, pp. 242, 467–72; T. Frame, *The Garden Island*, Kangaroo Press, Kenthurst, NSW, 1990, pp. 188–91, 193, 199–200.

18 Mellor, pp. 471–2.

19 Booklet, *Establishments of the Department of Defence Production* (1956), section on

the CGEW, pp. 3–4: Office of Defence Production records held by ADI; Mellor, p. 461.

20 *A Summary . . . of Munitions Production*, p.1059.

21 ibid.

22 G.H. Gill, *The RAN 1939–42*, AWM, Canberra, 1957, pp. 5, 13, 32–3; Mellor, pp. 43, 339.

23 Mellor, p. 338; Department of Productivity report, 'Munitions Policy study:, c.1979, p. 15, ODP; *A Summary . . . of Munitions Production*, p. 1057.

24 L. McLean, *The History of Ordnance Factory Maribyrnong 1923–93*, privately published, 1993, p. 36.

25 Mellor, p. 83.

26 Booklet, *Establishments of the Department of Defence Production*, section on the OFB, p. 4; Mellor, p. 242.

27 *Establishments of the Department of Defence Production*; Mellor, p. 243.

28 Mellor, pp. 282–92.

29 Mellor, pp. 293. See also S.J. Butlin and C.B. Schedvin, *War Economy 1942–45*, AWM, Canberra, 1977, pp. 69–70.

30 Mellor, pp. 294–300.

31 *A Summary . . . of Munitions Production*, p. 1059.

32 Mellor, p. 430, 446–8.

33 G.R. Worledge, ed., *Contact!: HMAS Rushcutter and Australia's Submarine Hunters, 1939–46*, A/S Officers' Association, Sydney, 1994, p. 53.

34 Mellor, p. 466; Worledge, p. 53.

35 L. McAulay, *Battle of the Bismarck Sea*, St Martin's, NY, 1991, p. 15.

36 P. Hasluck, *The Government and the People, 1939–41*, AWM, Canberra, 1952, pp. 603, 607.

37 B. Loxton with C. Coulthard-Clark, *The Shame of Savo*, Allen & Unwin, Sydney, 1994, p. 56.

38 M. McKernan, *All in!: Australia during the Second World War*, Nelson, Melbourne, 1983, pp. 66, 142, 177–8, 227–31.

39 Booklet, *Establishments of the Department of Defence Production*, section on the OFB, p. 5.

40 Mellor, p. 294.

Chapter 6   The Royal Australian Navy in the Mediterranean in World War II

1 The Chatfield Papers, National Maritime Museum, Greenwich, provide examples of the RN's attitude to the alienation of Italy.

2 Cunningham Papers, British Museum.

3 G.H. Gill, *The RAN 1939–45*, vol. I, Collins, Sydney, 1985, p. 75.

4 ibid. p. 137.

5 J. Collins, *HMAS Sydney*, Naval Historical Society of Australia (NHSA), 1971, p. 9.

6 Commissioned Gunner J.H. Endicott, an RN officer on loan, killed by splinters.

7 Collins, p. 17.

8 ibid. p. 18.

9 The Walrus aircraft had been damaged by bombing during the Battle of Calabria. Gunnery figures from Cunningham's report, ibid. p. 19.

10 Gill, p. 237.

11 A. Payne, *HMAS Perth*, NHSA, 1978, pp. 23–4.

12 ibid., p. 288.

13 For *Stuart's* modifications after the Malta refit see, R. Gillett, *Australian and New Zealand Warships*, Doubleday, Sydney, 1983, pp. 100–1

14 Gill, p. 297.

15 ibid., p. 293.

16 For an excellent account see J. Goldrick, 'Matapan', in *Great Battles of the RN*, ed. E. Grove, Cassell, London, 1994.

17 Gill, p. 315.

18 Goldrick, p. 203.

19 Gill, pp. 332–3

20 L. Lind & M. Payne, *'N' Class*, NHSA, 1974, pp. 1–3.

21 Gill, p. 364.

22 J. Neidpath, *The Singapore Naval Base and the Defence of Britain's Eastern Empire 1919–41*, Clarendon Press, Oxford, 1981, pp. 174–6.

23 Gill, pp. 391–2. These figures have been questioned, but seem credible to the author. The runs were eleven from Alexandria and nine from Mersa Matruh; eight to Alexandria and eleven to Mersa Matruh; the ship was on this duty without intermission from the end of May 1941 to the first week of August.

24 ibid.; p. 395.

25 For a recent discussion see D. Day, *The Great Betrayal*, Angus & Robertson, Sydney, 1988.

26 C. Barnett, *Engage the Enemy More Closely*, Norton, London, 1991, chap. 16.

27 Lind, pp. 102–11.

28 M. Van Crefeld, *Supplying War*, Cambridge University Press, 1977, chap. 6.

Chapter 8   South-West Pacific Sea Frontiers: Seapower in the Australian context

1 See J. Robertson, *Australia Goes to War*, Doubleday, Sydney, 1984, p. 215 and introduction to G.H. Gill, *The RAN 1939–45*, Collins, Sydney, 1985.

2 'Operational Control comprises those functions of command involving composition of task forces or groups or units, assignment of tasks, designation of objectives and coordination necessary to accomplish the mission'. Message, COMINCH to Admiralty 102212Z Feb. 1944, MP1587/1 296U, AA.

3 Directive to Supreme Commander SWPA, 15 Apr. 1942, A59543/1 Box 563, AA.

4 G.H. Gill, Papers of the Official Historian, AWM 69, no. 82.

5 Letter, Navy Office 030683, 3 Jun. 1942, MP1049/5 2026/14/279, AA.

6 Message, CANFSWPA to ACNB, 120615Z Sep. 1942, AWM 69, no. 82.

7 GOC New Guinea Force would be informed of the loading of ships by a combined US–Australian Army Cargo committee. As far ahead as possible, NOIC North-Eastern Area informed NOIC Port Moresby the dates when ships would be ready for call forward. NOIC Port Moresby then informed NOIC North-Eastern Area the dates ships were required at New Guinea ports by GOC New Guinea Force. Ships would then

be sailed by NOIC North-Eastern Area to arrive at times desired. Letter, CANFSWPA to CSWPSF, 18 Mar. 1943, MP1049/5 1844/2/12, AA.

8 By Sep. 1945, 450 200 Australian personnel had been transported without loss from Australia to ports north. MP1587/1 IT296B, AA.

9 AWM 69 no. 82.

10 Another six vessels were sunk in 1942 while not in convoy.

11 CSWPSF Summary of Shipping movements, Naval Historical Section (NHS) Canberra.

12 Memo., HQCinC US Fleet Convoy and Routing Section (USFCRS), 3 May 1943, MP1049/5 1844/2/12, AA.

13 Letter, CANFSWPA to ACNB, 4 Mar. 1943, MP1049/5 1844/2/12, AA.

14 The SWPSF Area was thus based on the SWPA, although the 'CHOP' line where merchant shipping moved from one area of control to another was adjusted from 110 degrees east to 100 degrees east. Letter, CANFSWPA to ACNB, 16 Mar. 1943, MP1049/5 1844/2/12, AA.

15 Letter, CANFSWPA to ACNB, 16 Mar. 1943, ibid.

16 SWPSF Merchant Shipping Instructions, 1 Jan. 1945, NHS.

17 Minutes, Advisory War Council (AWC), 9 Feb. 1943, A2682 vol. VI, AA.

18 RAN Daily Narrative, 28 Apr. 1943, NHS; minutes, AWC, 13 May 1943, A2682 vol. VI.

19 Minutes, AWC, 13 May 1943.

20 AWM 188 no. 28.

21 Eastern Area Operational Bulletin (EAOB), no. 1, Jun. 1943, 1969/100/2, Box 5, 6/5/9, AA.

22 Letter, CTF 78 to COM 7th Fleet, 27 Jun. 1943, MP1049/5 1932/3/31, AA.

23 Minutes, AWC, 3 Jun. 1943, A5954/1 531/5, AA.

24 Letter, *Rushcutter* to ACNB, 5 May 1943, MP1049/5 2026/12/537, AA.

25 Cases had occurred where convoys had to reduce speed so that the A/S vessels could maintain station. ibid.

26 M. White, *Australian Submarines*, AGPS, Canberra, 1992, p. 175.

27 G. Worledge, ed. *Contact! HMAS Rushcutter and Australia's Submarine Hunters*, The A/S Officers' Association, Sydney, 1994, p. 33.

28 Memo., USFCRS, 3 May 1943.

29 EAOB, Jul. 1943, AA1969/100/2 Box 5, 6/5/9, AA.

30 Memo., USFCRS, 3 May 1943. This difficulty was blamed for the loss of an opportunity to sink an apparently damaged Japanese submarine on 18 June 1943. CSWPSF had directed that measures were to be taken to search the area off Coffs Harbour after a torpedo attack on a convoy and a convincing depth charge attack by *Warrnambool*. RAAF Beauforts were ordered out by AOC Eastern Area on a creeping line ahead search. A submarine on the surface was sighted and attacks were made by two aircraft, but attempts to alert the three naval vessels in the vicinity failed after a complete failure to establish communications. Nevertheless, there is some doubt as to whether it was actually a submarine that was attacked. D. Stevens, '*I–174*', *Journal of the AWM*, no. 22, April 1993, pp. 35–41.

31 Minute, Area Intelligence Officer to AOC RAAF Command, 22 May 1943, 1969/100/2, Box 5, 6/2/22, AA.

32 Letter, AOC to CSWPSF, 16 Jul. 1943, ibid.

33 Letter, CANFSWPA to CSWPSF, 10 May 1943, MP1049/5 1932/3/31, AA.
34 Minute, DA/SD to CNS, 14 July 1943, ibid.
35 Two RAN specialist A/S officers were appointed to CTF 78 to assist with coordination of training in the North-Eastern Area. ibid.
36 Minute, DA/SD to DCNS, 2 Sep. 1943, ibid.
37 'The time is approaching . . . when sufficient escorts will become available to form escort groups and when this is achieved, and not until then, it will be possible to provide adequate and efficient convoy escort.' ibid.
38 Minute, DA/SD to CNS, 4 Sep. 1943, ibid.
39 Minute, DA/SD to CNS, 26 Jan. 1944, ibid.
40 Illustrating the rapidity with which the situation changed, LEUT L. M. Hinchliffe RAN was in mid-1943 posted to the Western Approaches Tactical Unit to gain experience prior to running a similar unit in Australia, where he would be required 'to combat the submarine menace'. Arriving back in Australia in August he was immediately sent on three weeks' leave. Worledge, p. 237.
41 Letter, Seamen's Union to Minister for the Navy, 13 Dec. 1943, AWM 69 no. 82.
42 Message, *BdU* to Penang, 141846Z Sep. 1944, FRUMEL CRS B5553/1, AA.
43 Message, CSWPSF to multiple addressees, 190900Z Sep. 1944, MP1049/5 2026/5/316, AA.
44 Message, CSWPSF to all mainland NOICs, 191358Z Sep. 1944, ibid.
45 Letter, NOIC Fremantle to ACNB, 25 Sep. 1944, ibid.
46 Now ADML T. Kinkaid USN, normally referred to as COM 7th Fleet.
47 Message, CinC SWPA to Allied Land, Naval and Air Forces, 281553Z Aug. 1945, MP1587/1 296, AA
48 Letter, Royle to Carpender, 18 Feb. 1943, MP1049/5 2026/10/1499, AA.

Chapter 9 The forgotten bases: The Royal Navies in the Pacific, 1945

1 The Naval Staff History on the War with Japan was an important secondary source. Volume VI of *Grand Strategy,* J. Ehreman, HMSO, 1956 in the British Cabinet Office Official History series provided useful background.

   Details of the Daniels Mission and the subsequent establishment of the administrative and logistics headquarters in Australia were provided by Vice Admiral (Q)'s Report (Appendix I to CinC BPF's final 'Report on the Experience of the BPF January–August 1945', 15 March 1946. Other details of the BPF's sea and shore logistics organisation are in the reports by Rear-Admiral, Fleet Train, and Commodore, Air Train.

   Volume III of the 'Submarine' Naval Staff History provides more details on the use of Fremantle, Subic Bay and Trincomalee.

   Personnel statistics are in Admiralty manpower returns and the programs for demobilisation are traced through a multitude of Admiralty Fleet Orders that identify individually thousands of officers and men scheduled for early release.

   The Admiralty War Diaries are a most useful source of information on the Admiralty's intent and achievement in the laying-up of ships in the UK and the movement of ships to the Far East. Port Movement Books, which provide a diary of arrivals and departures, range from excellent (Trincomalee) through fair (Fremantle) to virtually useless (Sydney).

Chapter 10 'Something peculiar to themselves': The social background of the Navy's officers in World War II

1 *Reflections on the RAN*, T. Frame, J. Goldrick, P. Jones, eds, Kangaroo Press, Kenthurst, 1991, p. 6.

2 C. McKee, *A Gentlemanly and Honorable Profession*, USNI Press, Maryland, 1991; D. Zimmerman, 'A Question of Identity: The Statistical Analysis of the Social Background of the Wartime Navy', unpublished, University of Canada, 1993; T. Mulligan, 'German U-boat Crews in WWII', in *The Journal of Military History*, vol. 56, no. 2, Apr. 1992.

3 G.H. Gill, *RAN 1939–45*, vol. I, Collins, Sydney, 1985, p. xiii.

4 ibid., pp. xi, 47–51.

5 McKee, p. ix.

6 F.B. Eldridge, *A History of the RANC*, Georgian House, Melbourne, 1949, p. 33.

7 A. Price, *Island Continent*, Angus & Robertson, Sydney, 1972, pp. 55–7.

8 F. Holt, *A Banker all at Sea*, Neptune Press, Newtown, 1983, p. 13; CRS MP981, 592/201/644, AA.

9 'Mnts of Conference on the Future of RANC held in HMAS *Australia*', under letter, CAPT Chalmer, Flag Captain to the RACAS, 23 Aug. 1929. RANC Historical Collection (RANHC), A.29.1.1.

10 Zimmerman, p. 22.

11 J. Grey, *Australian Brass: The Career of Lieutenant General Sir Horace Robertson*, CUP, 1992, pp. 80–1.

12 J. Grey, *A Military History of Australia*, CUP, Sydney, 1990, p. 150.

13 R. Bennett, *Australian Society and Government*, 5th edn., MM&B, Sydney, pp. 27–35.

14 J. McCalman, *Journeyings*, MUP, Carlton, 1993, pp. 4–5.

15 ibid., pp. 300–1.

16 *Report of the RANC for 1915*, Parliamentary Paper 308, vol. II 1914–17, Commonwealth Government Printer, 23 May 1916, p. 23.

17 Letter, RANC to Headmasters GPS, Apr. 1925, RANCHC, A.14.29.10.1.

18 'Report on Certain Aspects of Australian Defence', 20 Nov. 1934, Hankey Papers, ADFA.

19 Letter, CO RANC to ACNB, 26 Mar. 1928, CRS MP 981/1, 435/201/268, AA.

20 Gill, vol. I, p.48.

21 *Commonwealth of Australia Yearbook*, no. 32, Commonwealth Government Printer, 1939, pp. 176–83.

22 While service cards hold no information about the prior education of those joining the RAN, by using the Annual Reports of the College, reports of interviewing committees and other documents, it was possible to determine the schools attended by the boys of eleven entries between 1922 and 1940. 1922 & 1930, RANCHC A.14.29.10.1; 1923–28, RANHC, A.17.29.2.1; 1932, RANHC, A.15.27.6.1; 1938, CRS MP151, 465/208/522; 1940, CRS MP151, 265/208/539, AA.

23 C. Coulthard-Clark, *Duntroon*, Allen & Unwin, Sydney, 1986, pp. 274–5.

24 Letter, RANC to Headmasters GPS, Apr. 1925.

25 R. Thompson, *Religion in Australia*, OUP, Melbourne, 1994, p. 57.
26 Statement of the Government's Policy Regarding the Defence of Australia, 2 Dec. 1935, CRS MP124/6, 582/201/1367, AA.
27 McCalman, p. 168.
28 Coulthard-Clark, pp. 273–4.
29 McCalman, p. 169.
30 J. Collins, *As Luck Would Have It*, Angus & Robertson, Sydney, 1965, p. 1.
31 J. Leggoe, *Trying To Be Sailors*, St George Books, Perth, 1983, p. ix.
32 'Reflections of a Lower Deck Man', unpublished, NHS, Canberra, p. 13.
33 Letter, Sec. Naval Board to CO RANC, 18 Jun. 1921, CRS MP 472/1, 5/21/8149, AA; V.A.T. Smith, *A Few Memories*, ANI Press, Canberra, 1992, pp. 13–25; G.G.O. Gatacre, *A Naval Career*, Nautical Press, Manly, 1982, pp. 3–41.
34 Gill, vol. II, p. 710.
35 Frame, p. 7.
36 Holt, pp. 37, 140.
37 ibid., p. 240.
38 'Lower Deck Reflections', pp. 7–8.
39 H. Burrell, *Mermaids Do Exist*, MacMillan, Melbourne, 1986, p. 65.
40 P. Firkins, *Of Nautilus and Eagles*, Hutchinson, Melbourne, 1983, p. 220.
41 Grey, *A Military History of Australia*, p. 4.

Chapter 12   Vice-Admiral Sir John Augustine Collins, KBE, CB, RAN

1 Interview CMDR A.S. Storey (2nd 'G' in HMS *London*, ADML Horton's flagship) and CMDR R.P. Middleton ('G' in HMAS *Sydney*), Jun. 1992.
2 Letter, Collins to author, 21 Apr. 1976.
3 *Sydney*, ROP, Nov. 1939.
4 Admiral of the Fleet Viscount Cunningham, *A Sailor's Odyssey*, Hutchinson, London, 1951, p. 266.
5 Letter, RADM R.W. Paffard (secretary to ADML Tovey) to author, 15 May 94.
6 *Sydney*, ROP, Nov. 1940.
7 G. H. Gill, *The RAN, 1939–42*, AWM, Canberra, 1957, p. 432.
8 Interview with Lady Collins, Jun. 1992.
9 J. Collins, *As Luck Would Have It*, Angus & Robertson, Sydney, 1965, p. 100.
10 ibid. p. 101.
11 ibid. p. 103.
12 ibid. p. 105.
13 However, in *The Commanders*, David Horner made considerable but unsuccessful efforts to find someone to write Collins' biography.
14 Collins, p. 109.
15 Interview, I. Farquahar Smith (son of CAPT C. Farquahar Smith, DUO WA when Collins arrived), Jun. 1992
16 Hirst's service record.
17 Letter, RADM Griffiths to author, 1 Mar. 1993.
18 S.E. Morison, *US Naval Operations in WWII*, vols VII and XII, Little and Brown, Boston, 1951–58.

19 Interview, CMDR A.S. Storey (SO(O) CCAS Jun. 1944), 9 Jun. 1992.
20 P. Howson, *The Howson Diaries*, Viking Press, entry for 8 Jul. 1965, p. 163.

Chapter 14   The RAN Hydrographic Branch, 1942–45

1 Most of the material used derives from the author's personal records. Acknowledgment is made of the encouragement and assistance given by members of his family and, in particular, of material generously made available by Commander R.J. Hardstaff RAN (Retd). Verification of names, dates and events has been sought from the following documents:
G.H. Gill, *The RAN 1942–45*, Collins, Sydney, 1985.
Letters of Proceedings, HMAS *Warrego*, Mar.–Jul. 1945, AWM78 360/1.
Log Books—HMAS *Moresby*, Nov. 1943–Jan. 1945, AA.
G.C. Ingleton, *Charting a Continent*, Angus & Robertson, 1944.

Chapter 15   Touching on Fairmiles

1 Primary Sources include:
M.C. Hordern, War Journal 1942–46.
Notes and memoranda, Fairmile 'Defiant' Course, HMAS *Rushcutter* Aug. 1942.
Personal correspondence, 1942–46.
Secondary Sources include:
J. Lambert, *Allied Coastal Forces of WWII*, vol. 1, Conway, London, 1990.
Australian Sea Heritage, Magazine of the Sydney Maritime Museum, no. 11, Spring 1986 & no. 39, Winter 1994.

Chapter 16   The Royal Australian Navy in World War II: A Summary

1 J. Goldrick & A. Vincent, 'Australia', in *Ubi Sumus? The State of Naval and Maritime History*, ed. J.B. Hattendorf, Naval War College Press, Newport, 1994, pp. 23–4.
2 *Reflections on the RAN*, eds T. Frame, J. Goldrick, P. Jones, Kangaroo Press, Kenthurst, 1991.

Index

201

Women's Auxiliary Australian Air Force,
125, 132, 134
Women's Auxiliary Services (US), 133
Women's Emergency Signal Corps
(Australia), 124-5
Women's Naval Service (Australia), 124,
125
Women's Reserve Emergency Naval
Service (Australia), 124
Women's Royal Australian Naval Service,
10, 17, 124-34, *126,* 182

Women's Royal Naval Service (UK), 101,
102, 133
Women's Royal New Zealand Naval
Service, 133
Wood, Lieutenant 'Chips,' 170

Yachtsman's Scheme, 121
Yamamoto Isoroku, Admiral, 19, 20, 32
Yarra, HMAS, 75, 76, 87, 140
YMCA, 105
Yoichi Hirama, Rear-Admiral, 19

Zimmerman, D., 111